The Veteran's Millennium Health Care Act of 1999

A Case Study of Role Orientations of Legislators, the President, and Interest Groups

La Trice M. Washington

University Press of America,® Inc.
Dallas · Lanham · Boulder · New York · Oxford

University Press of America,® Inc.
4501 Forbes Boulevard
Suite 200
Lanham, Maryland 20706
UPA Acquisitions Department (301) 459-3366

PO Box 317
Oxford
OX2 9RU, UK

Printed in the United States of America
British Library Cataloging in Publication Information Available

Library of Congress Control Number: 2003111405
ISBN 0-7618-2665-3 (clothbound : alk. ppr.)
ISBN 0-7618-2666-1 (paperback : alk. ppr.)
ISBN: 978-0-7618-2665-1

DEDICATION

This book is dedicated to El Shaddai – the God of more than enough, I am eternally beholden to you for you are the source of my peace and joy. This project is also dedicated to my parents, Shirley and Howard, Sr., for their unconditional love, devotion, encouragement, and for having instilled in me a strong work ethic.

TABLE OF CONTENTS

PREFACE

This book is the product of my doctoral studies at Howard University. The research and writing of this case study took approximately one and a half years to complete.

My interest in veteran's issues, particularly veteran's health care benefits intensified during my employment with the United States House of Representatives. While working for Congresswoman Corrine Brown of Florida, I had the privilege of handling legislative issues in education, health care, Medicaid, Medicare, social security, aging and veteran's issues. I was also fortunate to have the opportunity to meet with veterans and lobbyists for veteran's interest groups to discuss the impact of veteran's entitlement programs and policies on their lives. It is through those meetings that I became familiar with veteran's organizations like the Paralyzed Veterans of America, Veterans of Foreign Wars, Vietnam Veterans of America, Jewish War Veterans and the like. Through communication and interaction with members of these groups, I became painfully aware of the health care needs, and daily struggles facing many veterans in the United States.

Furthermore, I became even more interested and impassioned about veterans entitlements when my uncle Ira M. Moses, Jr., a Korean War veteran, who served in both the U.S. Army and U.S. Navy died following a surgical procedure conducted at a VA hospital in Ohio. He suffered with lung cancer as a result of many years of smoking. He was convinced to undergo surgery to remove the most severely damaged lung in an effort to add several years to his life. During the surgical procedure the doctor removed the wrong lung mistakenly.

Following the operation, the family was informed that he was on life support and a decision needed to be made whether to continue such treatment. Eventually the family decided to have him removed from life support. Of course everyone wanted answers and no one had any. His death occurred during a time in which I was making a determination regarding the topic that would become my dissertation focus for the next sixteen to eighteen months.

Already familiar with the formulation of veteran's benefits from my professional experience handling veteran's affairs issues in the U.S. House of Representatives, I set out to research a bill titled "The Veterans Millennium Health Care Act" that was being considered during the 106th Congress. I quickly became aware of how extensive the history of veteran's entitlements was and found myself reaching as far back as to the Plymouth Colony.

The Holterman Fund of Otterbein College provided funding for various aspects of this project. I am immensely appreciative of the support offered by Dr. Brent Devore, and Dr. Patricia Frick at Otterbein. I am also very grateful to Dr. Allan D. Cooper and Dr. Debora Halbert for their feedback, support and encouragement. I appreciate the camaraderie of Dr. Sarah Fatherly, Dr. Lou Rose, Dr. Richard Yntema and Dr. Betsey McClain. I am tremendously indebted to Patti Welch for her technical assistance in preparing this manuscript for publication.

ACKNOWLEDGEMENTS

I especially want to express appreciation to my brothers, Lamonn, and Howard Jr., for teaching me not to take myself too seriously and for being a tremendous source of support. Your love, friendship, and camaraderie are priceless.

My heartfelt thanks go to Dr. Babalola Cole, my dissertation advisor, and professor. I am truly indebted to him for all of the support, advice, and direction he offered during this project. A special thanks goes to my committee members- Dr. Morris Levitt, Dr. Charles Harris, Dr. Maurice Woodard and Dr. Allan D. Cooper for their comments and guidance given to me throughout this dissertation.

To my aunts, uncles, cousins and extended family, thank you for words of encouragement and love. To my best friends Cassandra and Antonio Pettigrew, Sr., your support and love over these last fourteen years for is greatly appreciated. To my all of my teachers throughout the years, your commitment to the profession of teaching has bee an inspiration. Thank you for investing much time and effort into me. I have chosen to teach because of your passion, love and commitment to the profession.

CHAPTER 1

INTRODUCTION

This study examines the American legislative process, as it relates to the formulation and enactment of the Veteran's Millennium Health Care Act (VMHCA) of 1999 by the 106th Congress and President William Jefferson Clinton. The veteran's reform legislation was introduced in the House on June 9, 1999 and signed by President Clinton on November 30, 1999. This research discusses the various actors (legislators, congressional committees, interest groups, the president, bureaucrats, and health care providers, etc.) and their participation in guiding the legislation through the first session of the 106th Congress. The study utilizes two theoretical models designed by Malcolm Jewell and Samuel Patterson, i.e., "The Legislative Configuration System Model" and "The Legislative Role Orientation Model". These paradigms identify the actors involved in influencing the bill and highlight the existing relationship between the actors and the Congress.

The theoretical framework helps facilitate the identification of the behavior and activities engaged in by the above-mentioned actors. The theoretical framework also highlights the linkages that helped "fast-track" the enactment of the comprehensive veteran's entitlement package into law.

The primary goal of this study is to highlight the activities and tactics used by the various participants in the consideration and deliberation of the veteran's bill. This research also attempts to fill a gap that exists in the literature on the formulation and implementation of veteran's health care policies in the United States, which does not adequately address the influences of the participants and their relationship with the national legislature. Another goal of this study is to assist the reader in understanding the internal and external dynamics of veteran's health care politics in the 106th Congress. It is the intent of the author that this research will serve as an important document for public policymakers, lawmakers, and students of the American legislative process who desire to explore the dynamics surrounding the unprecedented swift passage of the veteran's health care reform bill. Finally, this study demonstrates the commitment of Congress to pursue important legislative needs of the nation, in a non-partisan or bi-partisan manner, even at a time of impassioned partisan conflict. In short, members of Congress successfully differentiated the needs of the nation while they were simultaneously embroiled in an attempt to impeach President William Jefferson Clinton.

This book is organized into six chapters. Chapter One introduces the reader to the purpose of the study, the statement of the problem, hypothesis, research questions, review of literature, theoretical framework, methodology, limitations of the study, significance of the study, and the piecemeal treatment and development of veteran's entitlements. Special emphasis is focused on veteran's health care benefits. Each subsequent chapter explores the influence of the participants in the legislative process as it relates to the Veteran's Millennium Health Care Act (VMHCA) of 1999.

Chapter Two treats the influence of President William "Bill" Clinton on the veteran's legislation. Information on the President's direct interaction with Congress and veteran's organizations was sparse; thus, the role and influence of Kenneth Kizer, Under-Secretary of Health for the Department of Veteran's Affairs and other key bureaucrats are dealt with as part of the President's bureaucracy.

Chapter Three analyzes the activities and strategies employed by the various congressional committees. Especial attention is paid to congressional hearings, markups, and proceedings of the House and Senate Committees on Veteran's Affairs that were involved in the consideration of the bill.

The involvement and influences of key congressional committee leaders within the Republican and Democratic parties during floor debates, like Representatives Bob Stump (R-AZ), Cliff Stearns (R-FL), Lane Evans (D-IL) and Senators Arlen Specter (R-PA), John

Rockefeller (D-WV) and Pete Domenici (R-NM), to name a few, are discussed in detail.

Chapter Four discusses the influences of interest groups, i.e., the American Legion, Jewish War Veterans, Paralyzed Veterans of America, the Vietnam Veterans of America, and state health care administrators, on the politics of the enactment of the Veteran's Millennium Health Care Act (VMHCA). The role of these pressure groups is significant to understanding the drafting of the original bill and its eventual passage. The movement and interaction of these groups is studied through the testimony they provided in committee hearings and proceedings. Furthermore, addition strategies (i.e., annual legislative presentations, litigation against the Department of Veteran's Affairs, and grassroots lobbying) used by the previously mentioned groups to influence the development and passage of House bill H.R. 2116.

Chapter Five discusses key stipulations of the new law P.L. 106-117 and its future impact on the provision and implementation of veteran's health care benefits in the United States. The final chapter consists of research findings on the role orientations of legislators, the president and veterans groups in the formulation and enactment of the Veteran's Millennium Health Care Act of 1999.

Problem Statement

The United States is required by law to provide veterans with benefits such as medical treatment, access to VA operated facilities, and pensions. The financial burden for the provision and maintenance of veteran's health care and other benefits is steadily increasing. This is particularly true in the case of veteran's services for those who suffer from "service-related" illnesses and chronic illnesses. This is explained by the fact that advances in technology and medical sciences have greatly prolonged the life expectancy of people. Furthermore, the number of veterans who are beneficiaries of veteran's programs in the United States has steadily increased. Paradoxically, the prolonged life expectancy of veterans has not been accompanied by an increase in the financial resources directed towards veteran's programs. For example, the Veteran's Administration (VA) reports that VA spending outlays for the fiscal years 1977 and 1996 increased by one hundred and three percent. The report also indicates an increase of ninety-eight percent in veteran's income security spending during the same period.

Additionally, federal spending for all other income security programs increased by two hundred eighty-four percent.[1] Although the Department of Veteran's Affairs (VA) is responsible for the delivery of health care services and benefits for veterans, congressional budget appropriations have not provided adequate funding for their implementation. Therefore, it is questionable whether adequate standards of health care assistance can be sustained in the future without dramatic increases in budgetary funding for veteran's entitlement programs.

Background

Throughout history, nations have developed programs aimed at assisting veterans coping with the illnesses and problems associated with having fought in a war. The United States actually began to develop assistance programs to deal with the problems afflicting veterans when the republic was still in its infancy. In fact, the Pilgrims for the Plymouth Colony following the war with the Pequot Indians in 1636 started the first veteran's assistance program.[2]

Since the above named year, there has been an ever-growing emphasis placed on issues that affect veterans. Americans have been involved in wars ranging from the American War of Independence through the Civil War, Vietnam War, the Persian Gulf War, and the more recent war against the Serbs. These wars resulted in an increasing number of war veterans who are in need of psychological, social, and medical assistance. In fact, as of July 1998, it was estimated that there are approximately 25.6 million veterans in the United States. Of this number, 19.3 million served in at least one war.[3]

In addition to the above programmatic problems, the United States is experiencing a shortage in available medical personnel. These two matters are therefore symptomatic of the difficulty confronting the VA and its health care delivery system. For example, the ratio of veteran to medical personnel is approximately 1 to 100,000. This creates a serious dilemma in providing effective medical treatment for America's veterans under constraining resources.[4] In fact, this situation has actually led to a type of medical rationing viz, veterans are not compelled to have annual or semi-annual physical examinations. Many veterans only see a medical professional when they are acutely ill. This approach to health care provides a compelling justification as to why many veterans suffer from chronic and life threatening illnesses. The competing objectives of providing effective and quality medical services to veterans against limited financial resources are difficult to reconcile.[5] This reality coupled with the fact that the Omnibus Reconciliation Act of 1990 placed restrictions on veteran eligibility for disability pension. The Act required, for the first time in the history of the program, that veterans be "fully" disabled in order to receive disability pension. Thus, veterans were required to prove that they were unemployable due to a service related illness. Furthermore, in 1997 as an attempt to decrease federal spending, Congress and President Clinton placed a "freeze" on the Department of Veteran's Affairs appropriations, which resulted in a decline in available medical services. While the law itself stipulated that veterans were entitled to medical treatment in VA operated facilities, veterans programs were not fully implemented due to the lack of adequate revenue. Over a nine-year period, from 1990 to 1999 and the enactment of the 1999 veterans legislation, incidences of chronically ill veterans increased dramatically nationwide because many did not receive medical services for their ailments. The failure of Congress and the president to increase appropriations to the department greatly contributed to the situation. The lack of adequate funding has undoubtedly had an adverse impact on the quality of life veterans experience, the provision of health care services, as well as their overall life expectancy rate. It is for these reasons that in 1999 Congress passed and President William Jefferson Clinton signed into law the Veteran's Millennium Health Care Act.

Hypothesis

The basic hypothesis for this study is where there is effective bipartisan cooperation and there is effective support by major interest groups, public policy is swiftly enacted.

Research Questions

This paper addresses the following research questions: (1) What factors facilitated the swift passage of the Veteran's Millennium Health Care Act, (2) Which committees and subcommittees were involved in the passage of the legislation, (3) What role did the president and high ranking bureaucrats play in the formulation and passage of the veteran's bill, (4) What was the role of interest groups in the passage of the Act, (5) What impact does the legislation have on veteran's entitlements, and (6) What lessons can be learned from the interaction of veteran's groups with Congress and the executive branch?

History of Veteran's Entitlement Programs

The United States government, through the Department of Veteran's Affairs, administers billions of dollars annually in federal benefits for military retirees, eligible veterans, and their dependents that now make up approximately one-third of the population. Because of the magnitude of these programs, the department operates hundreds of medical facilities, administers one hundred and fifteen national cemeteries, and issues millions of checks for education, disability, and pension.

During the early years of America's history, the colonies provided pensions for disabled veterans. The first law regarding this matter was enacted as early as 1636 by the Plymouth Colony. The colony provided money to individuals disabled in the colony's war against the Pequot Indians.[6]

In 1776, the Continental Congress sought to encourage enlistments in military service and curtail desertions from war and military service by enacting the nation's first pension law. The statute granted, "half pay for life" to individuals who lost a limb or suffered a serious disability in defense of their state. However, the Continental Congress did not have the authority or the money needed to make pension payments. Therefore, actual benefit payments devolved on the individual states. The Congress of the United States embodied the 1776 law in its first federal pension Act of 1789 and specifically provided that the federal government would "assume the burden" of providing veteran's benefits. Subsequent laws passed included provisions for those who fought in the War of 1812 as well as their dependents and survivors. In fact, due to an increase in the standard of living, cost of living and a surplus in the U.S. Treasury, Congress raised allowances for all disabled veterans and granted half-pay pensions for five years to their widows and orphans.[7] These early laws laid the foundation for the rationale that the nation owed a great debt to veterans, their spouses, and children.

Equally important is the Service Plan Act of 1818, which introduced the idea of providing pensions to veterans based on need. This law required that veterans of the American War of Independence who were in need of assistance would receive a fixed pension for life. In addition, enlisted men received eight dollars a month while officers received twenty dollars a month. Both the 1776 and 1818 laws marked a major shift in policy because all prior laws only provided pensions for disabled veterans. As a result, the number of veterans, which was 2,200 in 1816, had increased by 1820 to 17,730. Subsequently, the cost of pensions rose from $120,000 to $1.4 million. The cost associated with administering pensions, further grew when, in 1858, Congress authorized half-pay pensions to be paid to widows of veterans and their dependent children until they reached the age of sixteen. In order to administer the growing "programs," Congress authorized the establishment of the Bureau of Pensions as part of the Department of War in 1833. From 1840 to 1849, the Bureau was under the supervision of the Office of Pensions in the office of the Secretary of the Navy. It was later transferred to the Department of the Interior and renamed the Bureau of Pensions. Because of the foregoing, when the Civil War began in 1861, the country had approximately 80,000 war veterans. By the end of the Civil War, the number had increased from 80,000 to 1.9 million. This number does not include veterans who fought in the Confederate Army because they did not become eligible for federal benefits until 1958.[8]

Significantly, the General Pension Act of 1862 provided disability payments to veterans based on rank and the degree of disability rather than on the 1818 "Service Plan" law that existed before this date. The 1862 law covered military service in peacetime as well as the Civil War. For the first time in American history, the Act included compensation for diseases such as tuberculosis incurred while in service.[9] In addition, to the General Pension Act, the Homestead Act of 1862 provided Western land at a price of $1.25 an acre to veterans. It is important to note that the year 1862 marked the establishment of the National Cemetery System, which provided burial places for Union veterans of the Civil War.[10]

In 1812, the federal government began to provide medical care for disabled veterans in the United States by establishing the Navy Home in Philadelphia, Pennsylvania. Shortly thereafter, two additional medical facilities were established in the nation's capital, Washington, DC: The Soldiers Home and Saint Elizabeth's Hospital in 1853 and 1855, respectively.[11] The provision of health care treatment for disabled veterans and the establishment of medical facilities specifically for veterans created a precedent for the government assuming responsibility for the health condition of sick and wounded veterans.

The Consolidation Act of 1873 revised pension legislation by providing that subsidies must be based on the degree of disability as opposed to rank. It also authorized the aid and attendance program, which paid disabled veterans to hire a nurse or a housekeeper.[12] However, the Dependence Pension Act of 1890 broadened the scope of eligibility by providing pensions to veterans incapable of performing manual labor jobs. As a result, Civil War pensions were granted to servicemen discharged from the military due to illness or disabilities directly attributable to their military service.[13]

Congress continued to revisit the veteran's issue and decided, in 1912, to establish an overall pension system by enacting the Sherwood Act. Under it, all veterans were made eligible for pension. Furthermore, the statute allowed veterans of the Mexican War and Union veterans of the Civil War to automatically receive a pension upon reaching the age of sixty-two, regardless of their health status.[14]

In 1919, responsibility for medical care of veterans was placed in the Public Health Service. This change in policy transferred a number of military hospitals to the Public Health Service and authorized the construction of new hospital facilities. Despite the creation of additional health facilities, it was difficult for the Public Health Service to keep up with the increasing workload. Consequently, the law allowed it to award contracts to private hospitals to provide needed services to veterans.[15]

In 1929, President Herbert Hoover proposed, in his State of the Union Address, consolidating the disparate agencies administering veteran's benefits. Congress acted on the President's proposal and enacted a law that created the Veteran's Administration (VA). The law also consolidated the Veteran's Bureau, the Bureau of Pensions, and the National Home for Disabled Volunteer Soldiers into one administrative agency. President Hoover signed an Executive Order officially establishing the Veteran's Administration on July 21, 1930.[16]

During the Great Depression (1929-1934), demand for hospital care for veterans rose drastically. The increase in the number of hospitalized veterans was necessitated by incidences of tuberculosis and other related illnesses. The number of VA hospitals increased from 64 to 91. In addition, the number of beds provided for hospitalized veterans rose from 33,669 to 61,849. As a result, President Franklin Roosevelt persuaded Congress to pass the "Economy Act" in March of

1933. The enactment gave the president the authority to issue new veteran's benefits. President Roosevelt, then radically reduced veteran's benefits in an effect to reduce the deficit and balance the budget. This represented the first effort by the federal government to retreat from the responsibility it had assumed in care for the nation's veteran's population. Following the Great Depression and Roosevelt's presidency, Congress reenacted most of the laws that had previously been passed.[17]

The Selective Training and Service Act of 1940 authorized the first peacetime draft and guaranteed reemployment rights to anyone who left a job to join the armed services. Following the attack on Pearl Harbor, Congress made "service-connected" disability policies more liberal. The Act also provided families of servicemen who had been killed or disabled to receive training if the veteran lacked life insurance. Furthermore, many physicians, nurses, and dentists were drafted for military service. In an effort to replace these persons in the workplace, the Veteran's Administration reduced the minimum age and physical requirements for employment. Consequently, women were hired for positions previously held solely by men.[18]

In 1944, the Servicemen's Readjustment Act known as the "GI Bill of Rights" was passed. This law, which dramatically transformed the idea of veteran's benefits, had three provisions. President Franklin Roosevelt signed it into law on June 22, 1944. First, the Act provided for up to four years of education or training. The education package included the payment of up to $500 a school year for tuition, fees, and books as well as a monthly subsistence allowance. Second, the program provided veterans with federally guaranteed home, farm and business loans with no down payment required. This feature was included to help generate jobs in the housing industry while simultaneously providing housing for veterans and their families. The third provision provided unemployment compensation. This program transformed both the United States and its economy. Dreams of higher education and home ownership became a reality for millions of veterans and their families. Moreover, the Veteran's Preference Act was another significant piece of legislation passed in 1944. It authorized the president to set aside government jobs for veterans for the duration of the war in which a veteran fought or for up to five years following the war. The Act required government administrators who declined to hire veterans to submit a written justification for their decision.[19]

Congress followed the "GI Bill of Rights" five years later with the Disabled Veteran's Rehabilitation Act. This statute established a vocational rehabilitation program for disabled World War II veterans who served after December 6, 1941. Consequently, the Veteran's Administration provided over 620,000 disabled World War II veterans with job training. Additionally, the law entitled veterans who were declared totally disabled to receive compensation in the amount of $150 per month. Veterans who were partially disabled during military duty received compensation based on the severity of the disability or injury sustained while serving in a war.[20]

In 1958, a permanent system of unemployment insurance was created and for the first time, legislation provided this form of insurance to peacetime veterans. In yet another move to address educational needs of veterans, Congress passed the Veteran's Readjustment Benefits Act of 1958, which restored educational benefits to veterans. The provision gave veterans who had been on active duty for more than 180 consecutive days an entitlement of one month of educational assistance for each month that they served.[21] Of equal importance was the passage of the Post-Vietnam War Veteran's Educational Assistance Act in 1979. This law was established for persons entering the military after December 31, 1976. It allowed a "servicemember" to contribute up to $2,700 towards an educational fund and the federal government to match the veteran's contribution by providing $2 for each dollar he contributed.[22]

Following the passage of the Veteran's Health Care Amendments of 1979, the Veteran's Administration began to set up a network of Veteran Centers throughout the United States. Much of the Veteran's Administration's efforts in the 1980s were devoted to providing services to homeless and chronically ill patients as well as responding to the incredibly large numbers of patients with Acquired Immune Deficiency Syndrome (AIDS). By 1997, there were approximately two hundred and six (206) centers providing counseling services and treatments for post-traumatic stress disorder. The Act also provided for programs to treat veterans confronting alcohol or drug dependency problems in community facilities.[23]

The 1990 Omnibus Budget Reconciliation Act placed limitations on eligibility for disability pension. Previous legislation classified low-income wartime veterans over the age of sixty-five as disabled. The 1990 Reconciliation Act applied to all claims filed after October 1990 and it required that in order to be determined completely disabled, a veteran of any age had to be considered unemployable because of a disability that was expected to persist throughout the remainder of his/her lifespan. In 1995, hospitals under the supervision of the Veteran's Administration were grouped into twenty-two Veteran's Integrated Service Networks (VISNs). This response was the VA's attempt to resolve matters surrounding changes in health care delivery. These changes were made based on information regarding population-based planning, decentralization, universal availability of primary care, a shift to out-patient care as well as an emphasis on measuring health-care performance on the outcome of patient treatment.[24]

The Veteran's Benefits Improvements Act, which was enacted in 1996, revised basic entitlement requirements for disabled veterans. It also ensured that disabled veterans received quality training and rehabilitation services. The Veteran's Administration (VA) was given the responsibility of providing job-readiness skills and counseling services to participating veterans as well as offering independent-living services under the Rehabilitation Act of 1973. Furthermore, it allowed rehabilitated veterans to receive a subsistence allowance for two months while completing a veteran's employment program. Additionally, the Veteran's Benefits Improvements Act of 1996 extended educational benefits under the "GI Bill" for any member of the Army or Air National Guard whose duty began after June 30, 1985. Lastly, the Act contained provisions for employment and training, life insurance programs and other services to assist veterans in making the transition from military life to civilian life.[25]

The Veteran's Compensation Cost-of-Living Adjustment (COLA) Act of 1996 was enacted to increase disability compensation, compensation for dependents, clothing allowances and dependency and indemnity compensation for veterans and their dependents. It required the Department of Veteran's Affairs to increase the percentage in benefits at a rate equal to increases under the Social Security Act. It further mandated that the Department of Veteran's Affairs state the increases in veteran's compensation in the Federal Register when information regarding increases in Social Security benefits were published.[26]

In November 1999, one month before the start of new millennium, the Veteran's Millennium Health Care Act (VMHCA) was enacted. The legislative measure was designed to expand long-term care services for veterans including nursing home care, community based services and respite care. The law authorized increased access to health care facilities and services provided by the Veteran's Administration (VA). Furthermore, the Act granted higher priority access to VA medical services for military retirees despite their previous placement in the priority system, which governed veteran access to the Veteran's Administration's health care services. For example, veterans who were awarded the Purple Heart were given priority access to free, higher priority health care.

Moreover, the Veteran's Millennium Health Care Act (VMHCA) required the Veteran's Administration to consider alternatives to acquiring funds and to utilize these funds to offset budgetary shortfalls. The rationale for the provision was based on the need for the VA to begin to independently raise revenue and reduce its dependence on federal appropriations for its operating costs. For example, the Act allows the Veteran's Administration to increase co-payments for items such as prescription drugs and hearing aids. This measure was included in the Act as a means of allowing the administration to build capital while financing a major portion of the bill for veteran health care in the United States.[27]

Literature Review

This section of the study deals with: (1) a general review of literature on the American Legislative Process, (2) the literature on the role of the executive branch and its agencies in influencing the passage and implementation of the law and its provisions, (3) literature on the roles and functions of legislators and congressional committees, and (4) the relevant literature on the role of interest groups and public opinion in the formulation and passage of the Act.

There is an extensive body of literature on the legislative process, which primarily focuses on the policy, programs, and national institutions. Such literature tends to treat the branches of government in a distinctively separate fashion. This section of the study reviews the literature that is applicable to the general nature of politics, the influence of members of Congress, the executive, political parties and interest groups that wield power, and influence in the legislative process.

Numerous literary and scholarly materials have been published on different elements of the process. Among the outstanding sources in this field that warrant attention are Arthur Bentley's *The*

Process of Government and David Truman's classic work *The Governmental Process: Political Interests and Public Opinion.* Bentley's book *The Process of Government* suggests that the study of politics is incomplete without an examination of the crucial and distinctive role played by interest groups in United States politics. Thus, he directs the reader's attention to the interaction of interest groups within the political process.[28] Likewise, David Truman asserts the integral role of interest groups in politics in the United States. Interest groups are closely related to the daily functions of the political process - legislative, executive, judicial, and electoral process, campaigns, and elections. Therefore, it is virtually impossible to adequately describe the political process if interest groups are not included in the discussion. Unlike Arthur Bentley, Truman expands interest group theory to include and suggest the need for individuals to participate in these groups. David Truman contends that the desire to join interest groups lies in the very nature of human kind.[29]

Moreover, scholars such as Alan Rosenthal and Jeffrey Berry also offer detailed discussions of interest group politics as well as an examination of the tactics utilized by such organized groups. Both Berry and Rosenthal illuminate the manner in which interest groups operate as well as impart an understanding of how these groups affect the development of the political system like face-to face meetings, letter-writing campaigns, contributing to political campaigns.[30]

Not of any lesser importance is Christopher Deering's book *Congressional Politics* that highlights the manner in which Senators and Representatives participate in and influence the passage of legislation. Members of Congress engage in tactics such as carefully formulating or drafting bills, scheduling bills and committee hearings, coalition building and identifying external power brokers (i.e., interest groups). Additionally, Christopher Deering examines the role of congressional committees in the legislative process. [31]

In their work, *Committees in Congress* Christopher Deering and Steven Smith offer a detailed discussion of the composition and operations of congressional committees. The authors assert that committees possess and wield enormous influence on legislation within their jurisdiction. Consequently, they are able to shape and influence legislation. The authors also discuss in a detailed fashion the legislative operations of the committees in Congress. They maintain that there are two primary forms of power that are used by members of committees, namely negative power and positive power. Committees exploit negative power when they protect the status quo and fend off members who seek reform. In addition, committees posses negative power in their relationship with the full chamber. In this regard, negative power rests on the committee's ability to restrict the policy choices of the full chamber. The ultimate use of this power is in the committee's ability to decide not to report a bill to the floor; committee leadership may simply refuse to deal with a particular piece of legislation. Thus, the bill dies in committee. [32]

The authors of *Committees in Congress* maintain that subcommittee government has replaced committee government. The term subcommittee government is frequently used to describe the nature of congressional decision-making. As a result, the responsibility for the majority of legislative activity (i.e., hearings, mark-ups and debates) occurs in the smaller subcommittee sessions. The authors also noted that while government by subcommittees has not been institutionalized in both houses of Congress, the House of Representatives appears to be moving in that direction. However, committees in the U.S. Senate have been reluctant to form independent subcommittees. Additionally, Smith and Deering avow that the goals of individual members, the committee environment, and the committee agenda continue to play a significant role in shaping committee decision-making. Thus, shifts in the goals of the rank-and-file members generally have little or no effect on committee decision-making patterns. Yet, a change in the goals of the committee chairperson can swiftly alter the legislative functions performed by the committee.

David Truman's classic work, *The Governmental Process*, contends congressional hearings serve three functions. Hearings are crucial because they provide "a means of transmitting information, both technical and political, from various actual and potential interest groups" to the committee. They also act as "a propaganda channel through which a public may be extended and segments partially consolidated or reinforced."[33] Third, committee hearings act as a "quasi-ritualistic" mechanism that allows legislators to adjust to existing group conflicts to relieve disturbances. Legislators and witnesses alike recognize the usefulness of this ritual; it allows for the exchange of opinions and policy preferences.

In making their decisions, committees follow certain norms. Among the ones frequently used are reciprocity, apprenticeship, and specialization. The norm of practicing reciprocity requires non-subcommittee members to accept the recommendations of the subcommittee once the bill reaches the full committee. This norm is generally adhered to due to time limitations and the varying areas of specialization in Congress. Therefore, non-subcommittee members respect the decisions because subcommittee members possess the technical knowledge and skills to deliberate over the legislation. Apprenticeship in Congress requires that newcomers should spend time learning the committee norms, as well as their areas of jurisdiction. Because the norm of specialization grows out of the autonomy of congressional subcommittees, members who have served their period of training well, and are reelected receive important committee and subcommittee leadership positions. This norm also operates as the rationale of reciprocity and non-subcommittee members defer to their expertise.

Conversely, Edward V. Schneier and Bertram Gross in their book *Congress Today* also highlight the operations of committees in Congress. The authors emphasize that committee membership affords legislators the opportunity to share in the formulation of legislation through their ability to offer amendments. Furthermore, Schneier and Gross claim that the first task before a committee is to determine whether it should hold hearings on the bill. During congressional hearings, various groups, i.e. constituent groups, interest groups, experts, etc., offer statements, and testify before committees on legislative proposals. Frequently, the testimonies of these groups give committee members ideas for public policy.[34]

Richard Fenno in *Congressmen in Committees* addresses the function of congressional committees. The author maintains that the goals of members, committee agenda and political climate, play a role in shaping the decisions made by committees. Generally, rank and file members have little or no impact on the committee decision. However, he observes that any changes that occur in the goals of the chair of the committee can dramatically affect the function of the committee. Fenno argues that each member wants his committee service to be beneficial in terms of goals he or she holds as an individual member of Congress.[35]

In *Congress: The Electoral Connection*, David Mayhew argues that members functions with three basic goals in mind: (1) to be reelected; (2) to gain influence within the chamber; and (3) to make good public policy. He contends these objectives are widely held by members of Congress and are of the most consequence to committee activity. The author suggests that members affect public policy through leadership, partisanship, and participation and specialization. All of these elements affect the decision-making process in congressional committees.[36]

Forging Legislation, authored by Paul Light, illustrates the law-making process in the United States. His work provides a detailed and succinct discussion of the Department of Veteran's Affairs Act, which catapulted the Department of Veteran's Affairs to a cabinet level department. He uses a case study approach to studying the legislative process, more specifically "how a bill becomes a law." *Forging Legislation* provides the reader with an overview of the legislative process from the initial stage of agenda setting to the final passage of the bill. Furthermore, he provides a typology of styles of decision-makers: (1) the university teacher or rational actor who searches for truth; (2) the medieval warrior who pursues the exercise of unbridled power in an effort to emerge as a victor; (3) the businessman who acts as a policy entrepreneur; (4) the "garbage collector" who utilizes one bill in order to include issues that are likely to fail on their own merits; and (5) the small town neighbor who trades favors and makes decisions through the process of negotiation.[37]

In his book, *The Power of the Purse*, Richard Fenno examines the appropriations process from a case study of the House Appropriations Committee. Fenno contends that the internal political system in the House Appropriations Committee is governed by an "espirit de corp."[38] Thus, the author asserts that although committees are powerful, they fall short of being completely autonomous entities. This is partly because members of committees want to increase their influence in Congress. Therefore, Richard Fenno maintains that decision-making patterns can be explained by two variables: (1) the degree of respect and confidence the committee has developed in Congress due to its interaction with Congress as a whole; and (2) the degree of outside or external support which exists in the parent chamber.[39]

In his article "Concepts of Public Opinion," Francis G. Wilson argues public opinion is a very important element of political life. In a democratic society, public opinion adds value and legitimacy to government actions. The author suggests that public opinion increases the value of citizenship because it creates a sense of belonging. When a nation recognizes attitudes held by its citizens, public opinion can shape the attitudes demonstrated by others. Wilson speculates that public opinion is one of the most basic psychological foundations of the state. He emphasizes the importance of public opinion when the political attitudes expressed by the public are used to determine government actions. In addition, Francis Wilson suggests that members of society are entitled to their opinions. He points out that people, who reside in a democratic state, assume public opinion has influence. As such, public opinion is viewed as a mechanism of democratic control. Hence, public opinion is often viewed as the ethical foundation of a state. The author argues the "development of faith in public opinion coincided with the abandonment of authoritarian notions" of governance. However, when a natural bias is prevalently held in society, the function of public opinion is limited.[40]

In Public Opinion and Popular Government, Lawrence Lowell characterizes the "public" as individuals who are willing to abide by the decision of the majority. The author distinguishes several conditions that are critical to the existence of the public. He suggests that there should exist a sense of homogeneity of views on the treatment of questions. Second, Lowell declares that the public's response to questions must spur government action or inaction.[41]

The Chief Executive plays a significant role in the legislative process. George Edward's *Presidential Influence* and Richard Neustadt's *Presidential Power* both note that presidential power is critical to both the policymaking and the negotiation or compromise stage of the process. The authors assert that the President's arsenal is equipped with numerous weapons with which he could influence Congress. Among the available tools are the presidential reputation and the prestige that the position affords the Chief Executive. Consequently, the president has at his disposal crucial resources, which arm him with influence when engaging in the legislative process.[42]

In addition, White House liaison staff interacts with the Office of Legislative Affairs in an attempt to influence the direction of public policy and the formulation of new laws. John Hart argues in his article "Congressional Reaction to White House Lobbying" that the establishment of the White House Office of Congressional Relations (OCR) was an important development in the executive-legislative relations. The OCR follows the progress of bills in Congress, conveys White House interests and positions as a bill moves through subcommittees and committees, and gathers information on the intentions of members. Among the other valued services the Office offers is fulfilling congressional tour requests and providing information on available grants and grant awards. Accordingly, there are occasions when the White House can apply pressure on members of Congress. However, John Hart contends that it is difficult to measure the reaction of Congress to executive efforts aimed at influencing legislative issues. Furthermore, Hart maintains that occasionally White House liaisons have attempted to demand or dictate that legislators take a particular position on an issue or bill under consideration by Congress.[43]

V. O. Key in his book *Public Opinion and Democ*racy defines public opinion as attitudes held by the populace that compel the government to either act on or ignore particular issues. Depending on the popularity or homogeneity of a particular opinion, governments attempt to alter, pacify, or ignore public policy issues. Key insists that not all opinions expressed by the masses are regarded as public opinion. This holds true in cases where attitudes are widely embraced.[44]

In his article "Concepts of Public Opinion", Francis G. Wilson argues public opinion is a significant part of political life. In a democratic society, public opinion adds value and legitimacy to government actions. The author suggests that it also increases the value of citizenship because it creates a sense of belonging. When a nation acknowledges the attitudes held by it's citizens, it can shape the attitudes demonstrated by others. Wilson conjectures that public opinion is one of the most basic psychological foundations of the state. He stresses that it is important when the political attitudes expressed by the public are used to determine government actions. Furthermore, Wilson maintains that in order for public opinion to be embraced as a political force, people must believe that the government values it. Specifically, he states, "if public opinion is to be accepted finally as a political force, we must believe that opinion has value itself."[45]

In Public Opinion and Popular Government, A Lawrence Lowell defines the "public" as individuals who are willing to abide by the decision of the majority. The author identifies several conditions that are critical to the existence of the public. He suggests that there should exist a sense of homogeneity of views and the treatment of questions. Second, Lowell states that the public's response to questions must spur government action or inaction.[46] In addition, Walter Lippman, like Lowell, concurs that the essential problem with public opinion is participation. Lippman describes the public as spectators or "bystanders" who are interested in creating the rules by which the political game is carried out.[47]

In addition, Francis Wilson suggests that members of society are entitled to their opinions. He points out that people, who reside in a democratic state, assume public opinion has influence. As such, it is viewed as a mechanism of democratic control and it is often viewed as the ethical foundation of a state. The author argues the "development of faith in public opinion coincided with the abandonment of authoritarian notions" of governance. However, he continues, when a natural bias is prevalently held in society, the function of public opinion is limited.[48]

Theoretical Framework

This research utilizes the "Legislative Role Orientation" model and the "Legislative System Configuration" model designed by Malcolm Jewell and Samuel Patterson. The two models used make it possible to evaluate the flow of influence and linkages in the 106th Congress. They also assist in enhancing knowledge of the manner in which political systems function. In addition, the theoretical frameworks that are utilized provide excellent insight into the internal structural dynamics of the legislative process.

Malcolm Jewell and Samuel Patterson's Legislative Role Orientation model examines the relationships that exist between various influences in the Legislative Configuration System paradigm. The model incorporates a broad treatment of structural and functional systems analysis as the primary mode of analysis. The authors contend that decisionmaking in the legislative branch of government can be understood by examining the institutional environment in which the process occurs. Therefore, Jewell and Patterson assert that the institutional environment of the legislature is more than merely a collection of procedural and formal rules of organization. In fact, the authors argue that the legislative system is an extended social system in which internal and external actors interact with one another.[49]

Among the important concepts stressed by Malcolm Jewell and Samuel Patterson's paradigm are: the legislative system, legislation, and the legislation process. The term legislature is defined as a "collection of individuals who are elected as members of the formal parliamentary bodies prescribed by National and State Constitutions."[50] The authors highlight the role of interest groups, the

Chief Executive, political parties, and constituents in influencing and interacting with the members of the legislative branch.

Furthermore, Jewell and Patterson contend that the legislative system is made up of a number of actors who interact with one another in an attempt to achieve their social, political and administrative policy goals. It is precisely this system of interaction that the authors have coined "The Legislative System." The authors assert that the goals and relationships that are built and maintained are auxiliary concepts when studying the legislative process in the United States. Moreover, they suggest that in situations where members of the legislative bodies interact with individuals outside of the legislative structure, the latter enters the legislative system.[51]

Jewell and Patterson expand their legislative system and legislative process paradigm by formulating a theoretical framework, which explains how, demands and expectations of legislators are modified in an effort to influence the legislative output. The authors place the legislature within the context of a legislative input-output diagram. The inputs into the legislative system are the expectations, demands made, and resources offered by members of the executive branch of government, interest groups, and bureaucrats. The decisions reached are equivalent to system outputs or outcomes. Hence, system outputs include the formulation of bills and public policy as well as actions taken on pending legislation. The authors note that legislation need not be enacted into laws nor do services have to be provided to the public in order for an action to be considered a system output. Finally, Jewell and Patterson's theoretical model is completed by a "feedback loop" which indicates the continuity of the legislative system.[52]

Legislative roles, according to the authors, can be grouped into categories. Each category represents a different orientation and function on the state and national level. The role orientation model is divided into eight categories: (1) Legislative Role Orientation; (2) Bureaucratic Role Orientation; (3) Structural Role Orientation; (4) Representational Role Orientation; (5) Purposive Role Orientation; (6) Party Role Orientation; (7) Interest Group Orientation; and (8) Constituency Role Orientation. The authors view the legislature as a system in which roles are interrelated in a pattern similar to that of a network. They indicate that the roles of legislators, executive officials, party leaders, and constituents are interconnected in terms of their roles in the formulation and implementation of public policy.[53] The Legislative Role Orientation model is used to explain the role of congressional committees and committee leaders and the executive branch and its corresponding agencies in the passage of the Veteran's Millennium Health Care Act. It is through this model that one is able to examine the different roles played by congressional committees, their members, and the executive branch in the formulation of House bill H.R. 2116 - the Veteran's Millennium Health Care and Benefits Act of 1999.

Furthermore, the Legislative Role Orientation model is specifically applicable to these chapters because they directly examine the legislative process followed in the enactment of the Veteran's Millennium Health Care and Benefits Act and thereby the model is applicable to these chapters because each chapter deals with the institution of Congress and the manner in which it interacts with external actors, e.g., president, bureaucrats, interest groups, etc....

In the Bureaucratic Role Orientation model, legislators play the role of presidential spokesman when they are performing in an executive oriented fashion. However, when legislators view themselves as spokespersons of a government agency, they fulfill a role that is agency oriented. On the other hand, the Structural Role Orientation model suggests that legislators view themselves as either experts, committee members, leaders or individuals who have formed interpersonal relationships with their fellow colleagues in the legislative branch.[54]

In the Representational Role Orientation model, legislators make decisions based upon their individual conscience and the merits of the issue or legislation at hand. It is in this capacity, Jewell and Patterson argue, that legislators view themselves as delegates of those who elected them. When a legislator assumes the role of delegate, his or her decisionmaking is based on consultation with constituents and implementing the desires of his or her constituents. When a legislator functions as a delegate, he or she may be required to put his or her personal views aside if they differ from his or her constituents. On the other hand, a legislator may also express himself or herself as trustee by attempting to arrive at his or her own decisions based on his or her understanding of the issue or bill. Finally, the authors maintain that legislators may view themselves as both a delegate and trustee.[55]

In the Purposive Role Orientation model, legislators may view themselves as: (1) inventors, that is, they see themselves as formulating and initiating policy; (2) ritualists - they view themselves as involved in the technical routines of their work (i.e., committee participation and rules and procedures); (3) brokers - they assume the role of negotiating and coordinating legislation; (4) opportunists - they use their position and office to assume non-legislative roles; or (5) tribune - they view themselves as advocates of popular demands made by the public.[56]

In the Party Role Orientation model, the authors argue that legislators view themselves as a group whose role is to support their political party's policy preferences. Members of Congress also view themselves as individuals and independent units within the legislative system. As such, they frequently cross party lines if they believe that it is appropriate to do so. Furthermore, legislators view themselves as delegates and represent the interests of their constituency perhaps at the risk of appearing disloyal to their political party.[57]

The Interest Group Role Orientation model suggests that legislators may assume several roles when interacting with interest groups. The model suggests that legislators may act in a manner that is resistant to certain interest group tactics or activities. Furthermore, legislators may act as facilitators in which case they are aware of interest group activities to influence policy and welcome such group participation within the legislative process. Additionally, legislators may act in a manner that is neutral - neither favorable nor resistant to interest group activities.[58]

Finally, Jewell and Patterson observe legislators under the Constituency Role Orientation model. In this model, legislators view themselves as: (1) "Nation Oriented" -- legislators are extremely concerned with programs and policies that will benefit the nation as a whole; (2) "District Oriented" -- legislators support measures that will benefit their constituents and individual districts; or (3) legislators view themselves as both district and nation oriented and afford equal time to policies geared toward the interests of their respective districts and policies geared toward the interest of society.[59]

Methodology

The study utilizes a descriptive analysis approach in explaining the legislative process illustrated in the formulation and passage of the Veteran's Millennium Health Care Act (VMHCA) of 1999. It examines the roles and influences of various actors in the legislative structure in shaping the Act during the 106th Congress through the theoretical paradigms developed by Malcolm Jewell and Samuel Patterson. Furthermore, the models facilitate the examination of the influence of members of Congress and committees, the Chief Executive-President and bureaucrats from various executive departments, and interests groups.

In an effort to examine the activities of actors within the legislative system, this study utilizes both primary and secondary sources. The primary sources include: committee hearings and mark-ups, the *Congressional Record*, the *Congressional Daily Digest*, committee reports, presidential addresses and the various versions of the Veteran's Millennium Health Care Act. In addition, Lexis Nexis Academic Universe database and public opinion polls are utilized to measure public opinion on veteran's benefits and the impact that such data may have had on the passage of the veteran's bill. The secondary sources utilized include: scholarly literature in the sub-field of Legislative Process, journal, and newspaper articles.

Malcolm Jewell and Samuel Patterson contend that Congress is the center of the legislative system. The authors maintain that the United States Congress interacts with various external actors. Christopher Deering in *Congressional Politics* asserts that in order to study the influence of Congress as an institution, one must understand the internal dynamics of the committee system. Deering argues that Members of Congress assist in the formulation and passage of legislation by strategically engaging in coalition building and reaching compromises with both internal and external actors in the legislative process.

The *Congressional Record* and *Congressional Digest* mentioned earlier, contain data on floor deliberations in both chambers of Congress and "extension of remarks" made by members of the United States House of Representatives and United States Senate. In order to analyze the role of Congress in the drafting and passage of the Act, testimony, and statements made in both chambers during the first session of the 106th Congresses are examined. Moreover, information on the role of key committee members like Representatives Stearns, Stump, Evans, and Senators Specter and Rockefeller are reviewed.

The executive branch plays a significant role in the legislative process as a policy initiator. George Edwards in *Presidential Influence* contends that presidential power is crucial to policymaking and the negotiation stage of the legislative process. He argues that the president possesses an arsenal that is equipped with various weapons with which the executive can utilize to influence members of the legislative branch (i.e., prestige, the presidential reputation and party affiliation). Consequently, the president can employ these tools in his role as a policymaker in the legislative process. The Chief Executive's role in shaping the Veteran's Millennium Health Care (VMHCA) bill in the 106th is examined by reviewing presidential speeches and addresses, briefings and messages. These primary sources will enable one to identify and describe the reaction of the president to policy issues debated in Congress. Sources that will be consulted on the president's reaction to the issue of veteran's health care and benefits include the *Congressional Quarterly Report*, *The Public Papers of the Presidents,* and the *Weekly Compilation of Presidential Documents.* The *Congressional Quarterly Report* contains weekly radio addresses, speeches, and press briefings of presidents.

In order to study the politics of the United States, one must examine the role and influence of interest groups in the legislative system. David Truman and Arthur Bentley in their respective scholarly works, *The Governmental Process*[60] and *The Process of Government,*[61] argue that interest groups play a significant role in the legislative process. Thus, the role of interest groups and interest group activities are examined through the testimony of various veteran's organizations as well as state agencies and organizations responsible for administering veteran's programs.

Finally, this study examines some news publications. Newspapers including the *Washington Post, U.S. Newswire, St. Louis Post-Dispatch, The Tennessean, Dayton Daily News, The Plain Dealer, the Arizona Republic, VFW Washingtonwire, and Stars and Stripes* were examined. These newspapers were selected because they are widely read by policymakers and lawmakers. These publications contain information on congressional and national developments and reactions to major policy issues. Hence, these news publications are excellent sources for identifying and measuring the roles played by policymakers in the passage of the Veteran's Millennium Health Care Act (VMHCA). Additionally, newspapers in geographical areas with large concentrations of veterans, i.e. Ohio, Arizona, Tennessee, etc., were consulted. These newspapers contain editorials and feedback on issues surrounding the drafting and passage of the Act, as well as the plight of America's veterans.

Limitation of Study

This study specifically examines the legislative process, as it relates to the passage of the Veteran's Millennium Health Care Act (VMHCA) of 1999 by the 106th Congress. Although this study includes a discussion of the roles played by various actors in the legislative process and the influence they wielded on the passage of the Act, it is not the writers intent to attempt to determine which actors were most influential in the passage of the Act because an attempt to do so would be speculative in nature. The examination does not involve quantitative analysis.

Significance of Study

The primary focus of this study is to investigate the legislative process as it deals with of the Veteran's Millennium Health Care Act (VMHCA) of 1999. The research is significant in that it fills the gap in existing literature on veterans health care entitlements which does not treat the roles played by various actors, i.e., members of Congress, interest groups, president, etc., in the legislation of veteran's health care issues, but rather focuses on the overall impact of the VA health care delivery system on the state of veterans health.

This work presents a discourse and documentation of the influence of the various actors involved in the legislative process of veteran's health care and benefits in the 106th Congress. It is the writer's belief this study will serve as an important document for students interested in exploring the dynamics of the legislative process, particularly veteran's legislation. This writer intends this study to also serve as an important document for lobbyists and lawmakers interested in developing a unique relationship with Congress like that, which exists between legislators and veteran's interest groups.

Finally, this research suggests that it is plausible for legislators to put their partisan differences aside during periods of great conflict between the political parties. This is illustrated in the behavior and role orientations of legislators, committees, Executive, and interest groups among others. Thus, this research also fills a void that exists in the literature by overly emphasizing conflict between the Democratic and Republican parties and the lack of focus given to the non-partisan function of legislators.

Notes

[1] U.S. Department of Veterans Affairs, Office of Public Affairs, *Facts About the Department of Veterans Affairs*, [Washington, D.C.]: U.S. of Veterans Affairs, Veterans Health Administration, 1999, 1.

[2] Ibid.

[3] Ibid.

[4] While most elderly Americans are eligible for Medicare, veterans enrolled in the VA health care program are not because the law prevents the use of both Medicare and VA health care system simultaneously. However, veteran's organizations such as the Paralyzed Veterans of America and the Vietnam Veterans of America all requested that Medicare subvention be provided to veterans in an effort to reduce the burden placed on the VA system and veterans. Nevertheless, Medicare subvention was not included in the new law.

[5] U.S. Congress, House, Committee on Veterans Affairs, Subcommittee on Health and Hospitals, Impact *of Budget Shortfalls on the Delivery of Health Care to Rural Veterans*, 100th Cong., 1st sess., 2 December 1988.

[6] U.S. Department of Veterans Affairs, Office of Public Affairs, *VA History in Brief* [Washington, D.C.]: U.S. Department of Veterans Affairs, Veterans Health Administration, 1998, 1.

[7] Ibid, 2. It was estimated that by 1816 2,200 veterans of that war were receiving such pensions.

[8] Ibid., 3-4.

[9] Ibid., 4

[10] *Homestead Act of 1962, Statutes at Large*, 12, secs. 75, 392(1862).

[11] Department of Veterans Affairs, Office of Public Affairs, *VA History In Brief* [Washington, D.C.]: U.S. Department of Veterans Affairs, Veterans Health Administration, 1998, 4.

[12] Ibid., 5.

[13] *The Dependence Pension Act, Statutes at Large*, 26, secs. 634,182 (1890).

[14] *The Sherwood Act, Statutes at Large,* 37, sec. 123, 112 (1912).

[15] Department of Veterans Affairs, Office of Public Affairs, *VA History in Brief,* [Washington, D.C.]: U.S. Department of Veterans Affairs, Veterans Health Administration, 1998, 7.

[16] Ibid., 11.

[17] Ibid.

[18] *The Selective Training Act, Statutes at Large,* 54, sec. 720, 885 (1940).

[19] *The Servicemen's Readjustment Act, Statutes at Large,* 58, secs. 268, 284 (1944).

[20] *The Disabled Veterans Rehabilitation, Statutes at Large,* 43, 607 (1949).

[21] *The Veterans Readjustment Act, Statutes at Large,* 72,, sec. 14 (101), 1273 (1958).

[22] *The Post-Vietnam War Veterans Educational Assistance Act, Statutes at Large,* 90, 2392 (1979).

[23] *The Veterans Health Care Amendments, Statutes at Large,* 93, 47 (1979).

[24] *The Omnibus Budget Reconciliation Act, Statutes at Large,* 104, secs. 102-123, 140, 301-305, 1388-236 (1990).

[25] *The Veterans Benefits Improvement Act, Statutes at Large,* 110, 3322 (1996).

[26] *The Veterans Compensation Cost-of-Living Adjustment Act, Statutes at Large,* 110, 3212 (1996).

[27] *The Veteran's Millennium Health Care Act, Statutes at Large,* 113, 1545 (1999).

[28] Arthur Bentley, *The Process of Government* (Bloomington: The Principia Press, Inc., 1935).

[29] David Truman, *The Governmental Process* 1st ed. (NewYork: Alfred A. Knopf, Inc., 1951).

---

[30] Alan Rosenthal, *The Third House: Lobbyists and Lobbying in the State* (Washington, D.C.: Congressional Quarterly Press, 1993) and Jeffrey Berry, *Interest Group Society* 2nd ed. (Boston: Little Brown and Company, 1989).

[31] Christopher Deering, *Congressional Politics* (Illinois: The Dorsey Press, 1969).

[32] Christopher Deering and Steven Smith, *Committee in Congress* (Washington, DC: Congressional Quarterly Press, Inc., 1984).

[33] David Truman, *The Governmental Process* (New York: Knopf, Inc., 1953).

[34] Edward Schneier and Bertram Gross, *Congress Today* (New York: St. Martin's Press, 1993).

[35] Richard Fenno, *Congressman in Committees* (Boston: Little Brown and Company, 1973). For additional discussion of the political climate in legislatures, see Clinton Rossiter's *Parties and Politics in America* (1960).

[36] David Mayhew, *Congress: The Electoral Connection* (Massachusetts: Yale University, 1974).

[37] Paul Light, *Forging Legislation* (New York: W.W. Norton and Company, 1992), 238-240.

[38] Richard Fenno, *The Power of the Purse* (Boston: Little Brown, 1966).

[39] Ibid.

[40] Francis Wilson, "Concepts of Public Opinion," *The American Political Science Journal*, vol. 27, no. 3 (June 1933):371-372.

[41] A. Lawrence Lowell, *Public Opinion and Popular Government* (New York: Longmans Green and Company, 1930).

[42] George Edwards, Presidential *Influence* (San Francisco: W.H. Freeman and Company, 1980) and Richard Neustadt, *Presidential Power* (New York: John Wiley and Sons, Inc., 1964). Additional treatment of the role of the president in the legislative process is covered in Clinton Rossiter's *The American Presidency (New York: Harcourt Brace, 1956),* Edward S. Corwin's *The President, Office and Powers, 1787-1948* (New York: New York University Press, 1948).

[43] John Hart, "Congressional Reaction to the White House," *Presidential Studies Quarterly*, Vol. XI (Winter 1980), 83-91.

[44] V. O. Key, *Public Opinion and Democracy* (New York: Alfred Knopf, 1961), 13-14.

[45] Francis Wilson, "Concepts of Public Opinion," *The American Political Science Review*, vol. 27, no. 3 (June 1933), 371-372.

[46] A. Lawrence Lowell, *Public Opinion and Popular Government* (New York: Longmans Green and Company, 1930).

[47] Walter Lippman, *The Phantom Public* (New York, Hartcourt Brace, 1925), 52.

[48] Wilson, 384.

[49] Malcolm Jewell and Samuel Patterson, *The Legislative Process in the United States* (New York: Random House, 1977), 3.

[50] Ibid.

[51] Ibid., 348.

[52] Ibid., 349-350.

[53] Ibid., 351.

[54] Ibid., 350-351.

[55] Ibid., 350.

[56] Ibid., 351.

[57] Ibid., 1.

[58] Ibid., 349-350.

[59] Ibid., 348.

[60] David Truman, *The Governmental Process* 1st ed. (New York: Alfred A. Knopf, Inc., 1951).

[61] Arthur Bentley, *The Process of Government* (Bloomington: The Principia Press, Inc., 1935).

CHAPTER 2

THE ROLE OF THE PRESIDENT

This chapter examines the role of the president and the executive branch in the consideration and enactment of the Veteran's Millennium Health Care Act (VMHCA) of 1999. The chapter also discusses various tools used by the president in influencing the veteran's agenda during the first session of the 106th Congress. In attempting to advance his political agenda, the president can employ a number of strategies, techniques, and tools to influence Congress. Many of the tools are based on legal authority or formal powers granted to the Chief Executive in the U.S. Constitution. Others are informal powers developed as the presidency matured. Furthermore, some are the result of a unique blend of these powers and the political astuteness and leadership ability of individual presidents. There exists a wealth of literature on the powers and strategies used by presidents in their attempts to carry out their political agenda.

The literature utilized in this section is primarily composed of congressional hearings, presidential weekly addresses, speeches, and statements of executive officials. In addition, this section examines testimony presented by members of the executive branch at congressional hearings held before the House and Senate Committee on Veteran's Affairs (e.g., Stephen Backhus, Director of the Veteran's Affairs and Military Health Care Issues and Kenneth Kizer, Undersecretary for Health with the Department of Veteran's Affairs).

Moreover, newspaper articles that depict the position of the Clinton administration on veteran's health care issues, specifically the Veteran's Millennium Health Care Act, were consulted.

The Chief Executive plays a significant role in the legislative process. The U.S. Constitution grants the president the power to approve or reject legislative matters passed by Congress. Article I, section 7 of the Constitution states that Congress must present to the president for his consideration all bills passed by the legislature. When there is agreement between the legislature and the executive on policy decisions, the president simply signs the bill. However, under Article I, section 7 of the Constitution, the president can veto legislative measures he does not support. In such an instance, he returns the legislative measure to Congress with an explanation of his objections.[1] Furthermore, the Constitution requires that the president communicate his legislative agenda, policy preferences, and policy recommendations to the legislature. In addition, he is given the authority to call special sessions of Congress and to adjourn it in times of disagreement.[2] These constitutional provisions give him the authority to participate in the legislative process.

In fact, the president plays the role of chief legislator and is expected to initiate legislation. Richard Neustadt's *Presidential Power* and George Edward's *Presidential Influence* in Congress both note that the president wields an enormous amount of power in the negotiation of public policy. The authors argue that the president's arsenal is equipped with numerous weapons that allow him to influence the national legislature. Among the tools often utilized by a president are presidential prestige and reputation. Consequently, these tools afford the Chief Executive an increased ability to assertively engage in the legislative process.[3]

Presidential Tools of Influence

The Chief Executive also has at his disposal executive personnel and bureaucrats who further assist in applying pressure on members of Congress. White House liaison staff interacts with the Office of Legislative Affairs on a daily basis in an effort to influence the direction of public policy and the formulation of new laws. The establishment of the White House Office of Congressional Relations was an important development in executive-legislative relations. Among the valued services, the Office offers are fulfilling congressional tour requests, providing information on available grants and grant awards. Therefore, on occasion the White House is able to apply pressure on members of Congress. However, Hart contends that it is difficult to measure the reaction of Congress to executive efforts aimed at influencing legislative issues. Furthermore, the author maintained that occasionally White House liaisons have attempted to demand or dictate that legislators take a particular position on an issue or bill under consideration by Congress.[4]

There exists a number of ways in which U.S. Presidents use legislative skills to influence public policy. He notes that Presidents Johnson, Kennedy, Nixon, and Eisenhower all frequently met with congressional party leaders to discuss pending legislation and programmatic issues. For example, he discusses the fact that President Kennedy held Tuesday breakfasts with the Democratic leadership of the U.S. House of Representatives and the U.S. Senate. He also notes that President Lyndon Johnson's staff worked closely with party leaders. President Johnson's staff attended strategy sessions held in the offices of party leaders, discussed legislative strategy and tactics as well as the merits or substance of pending legislation. Consequently, during Johnson's presidency, the White House developed and maintained a complimentary relationship with Congress.[5]

Furthermore, presidents often make personal appeals for votes or legislation. This tactic allows the president to directly appeal to the public, congressional leaders and members of both chambers in an attempt to shape the discussion and direction of an issue or bill. He suggests that the president may attempt to shape legislation or the vote on a bill by personally calling members of Congress on the telephone to express why he favors or opposes legislation. For example, the author points to Johnson's actions as extensive. President Johnson's persistence in searching for votes was extraordinary because the president accepted no as a response to his request for support. President Johnson would go to great lengths to ensure the outcome of a vote. The Chief Executive may also attempt to round up or gather votes to support or oppose a bill. For example, Edwards discusses how the president personally rounded up votes on issues including food stamps, poverty programs, federal pay increase and farm legislation. Likewise, President John F. Kennedy believed that maintaining personal contacts with Congress was imperative. However, some presidents are less likely to contact members of Congress to solicit votes.[6]

Nevertheless, despite the prestige of the office of president and the persuasiveness of the leader, presidents are not always successful in their personal appeals. In fact, despite the efforts of Presidents Eisenhower, Kennedy, and Johnson, occasionally the president failed to persuade members to support his position on public policy. Consequently, the author suggests that the political shrewdness of a president is not necessarily enough to dictate policy outcomes.[7]

Additionally, the Chief Executive attempts to facilitate negotiation or bargaining between groups in Congress. This tactic is utilized in an attempt to force the members to compromise with one another to achieve their legislative goals. For instance, President Kennedy included a broad range of educational programs in a 1963 omnibus education bill in an effort to encourage education organizations to resolve differences and work together. As an incentive, the omnibus bill included a measure that renewed financial assistance to federally impacted areas, which was embraced by the public school officials. Nevertheless, the number of deals that are reached in this manner must remain relatively low due to the scarcity of resources and the demand for such resources. Therefore, the majority of bargains reached in this manner are implicit due to the contempt associated with bargaining or traded favors. Fortunately, the president does not have to bargain with every member of Congress. Thus, the president need only bargain with enough powerful leaders (e.g., committee and subcommittee chairs and ranking members) to secure enough votes to secure a majority of votes. However, on occasion, the president is simply unwilling to bargain. For instance, in 1961, President Kennedy proposed closing a veteran's hospital in California in retaliation to Representative D. S. Saund's opposition to a provision in his foreign aid bill. The member was angered by the president's proposal to close the veteran's hospital in his district.[8]

Moreover, George Edwards points out that in many instances it is a member of Congress who requests a favor in return for supporting the president. He writes, "when the White House calls and asks for support, representatives and senators frequently ask about a request that he or she has submitted."[9] Normally, the request for a favor is linked to the members' constituents.[10]

Another tactic utilized by the Chief Executive is referred to as "arm-twisting." This term refers to coercive techniques such as pressure to conform to the president's views or the use of threats to gain support from congressmen. Some presidents utilize this tactic in trying to influence the legislative process. However, several of the responsibility for gaining congressional support is placed on White House staff.[11] Regardless of whether it is the president or White House staff that attempts to coerce members of Congress, members react negatively to "arm-twisting" as a means to influencing public policy. Consequently, this tactic is utilized as a last resort in critical votes.[12]

Frequently, presidents make special appeals for votes on certain policy issues. This tactic affords him the opportunity to make personal appeals to members of Congress. When the chips are done, there is no substitute for the president's own footwork, his personal negotiation, his direct appeal, his voice and no other's on the telephone."[13] The use of personal contact via the telephone is often effective. However, this method must be utilized with care. Otherwise, the usefulness of this form of personal contact loses its value. Presidents have from time to time failed despite the enormous effort made to persuade legislators to support his position on an issue.[14] Although President Clinton possessed the power and authority to influence the shaping of the VMHCA through use of the aforementioned tools, the literature suggests that he more heavily relied on the use of "public appeals."

Use of Public Appeals as a Tool

The president of the United States also has at his disposal a number of formal powers like delivering public messages, vetoing legislative acts of Congress, preparing federal budget. These legal authorities are not equally effective in enhancing the president's impact on legislative matters. Nevertheless, the use of public appeals can be a persuasive means by which the president gets Congress to address measures included in his legislative agenda.

President William Clinton used public appeals to communicate and influence the shaping of the veterans reform bill. The non-controversial nature of veteran's health care and benefit programs provided the president with an opportunity to share his health care reform preferences with Congress, interest groups, and the American public. The Veteran's Millennium Health Care Act presented President Clinton with the opportunity to achieve several of his health care reform objectives. Many of these objectives, i.e., long-term care, emergency care, increased access to treatment, etc., were included in Clinton's 1992 failed health care reform proposal.

The Clinton health care reform plan, spearheaded by Hillary Clinton, proposed that all Americans were entitled to health care insurance. A large part of the Clinton's campaign success was attributed to his campaign promise to reform health care. Initially the proposal received a warm reception from voters. However, despite the Democratic majority in the House and Senate, the proposal fell prey to criticism and disparagement.

According to the American College of Physicians (ACP), the plan failed because the White House Task Force charged with developing the proposal failed to consult physicians and health care professionals. The plan also failed to maintain its momentum because the ACP along with other health professionals rallied around discrediting the plan. Furthermore, the fate of the plan was sealed when the president stated that he would veto legislation that did not include universal health care coverage.[15]

Furthermore, Republicans led by Newt Gingrich (R-GA) withheld support for the health care reform plan. Gingrich and his fellow Republicans believed that defeating health care reform would guarantee a Republican victory in the 1994 congressional elections. This strategy paid off for the Republican Party in 1994. The party gained political control in the House of Representatives and the Senate. In addition, the Health Insurance Association of America invested in excess of $20 million to defeat the Clinton health care reform plan. Moreover, small businesses mobilized grassroots opposition to the plan. Small business owners feared the financial burden that was associated with implementing the proposed plan.[16] The Clinton health care reform plan contained the following major elements:

1. tax-financed funding of health care insurance for unemployed and destitute workers;
2. minimum coverage standards;
3. regulation of health care alliances by state governments;
4. insurance premiums would vary based on the type of coverage selected by workers, i.e., individual and family.[17]

Obviously, President Clinton was displeased with the failure of his health reform plan. However, he became aware of how difficult it would be to reform health care. Therefore, the failure of the Clinton administration's attempt to reform health care prompted the administration to take a more piecemeal approach to redressing health care concerns. In 1999, the president again focused his attention on health care reform issues.

Consequently, President Clinton addressed the 106th Congress and the nation in his "State of the Union Address." He shared his views on the state of health care in the United States. Clinton asked Congress to "invest in long-term care."[18] The president suggested that Congress pass legislation that would enable senior citizens to receive a tax credit of $1,000 to offset long-term care costs. The president pointed out that long-term care costs are escalating because people are living longer. He also noted "long-term care will become a bigger challenge with the aging of America."[19] Consequently, President Clinton challenged Congress to "do more to help families" deal with long-term care issues. In addition, the president suggested that the federal government assume the burden for caring for veterans. He argued that the government could afford to assume this burden due to its economic success.[20]

Furthermore, President Clinton noted that patients should have the right to see a specialist without going through a complicated process. The president urged Congress to ensure that all Americans be allowed to receive emergency treatment at hospitals in close proximity to their homes. He ordered that Medicare, Medicaid, and veteran's health care programs allow beneficiaries to receive emergency treatment. Additionally, in a bold move, President Clinton urged the Republican leadership in the 106th Congress to earnestly work with Democratic members to develop a "Patients Bill of Rights." Specifically, the president challenged Republicans and Democrats to "join together across party lines."[21]

President William Jefferson Clinton also highlighted his legislative agenda, which included measures to:

1. improve treatment of mental illness;
2. allow the U.S. Department of Justice to hold tobacco companies liable for costs incurred to treat citizens suffering from illnesses related to the use of tobacco products; and
3. allow the U.S. Department of Justice to use funds recovered from settlements with tobacco companies to expand Medicare coverage.[22]

One month after his "State of the Union Address," President Clinton participated in a roundtable discussion on long-term health care. Again, he emphasized several proposals aimed towards addressing long-term health care issues. Many of the measures discussed were included in his failed health care reform effort. The president highlighted proposals that would:

1. enable disabled and elderly people to receive a $1,000 tax credit to defray long-term health care costs;
2. establish a "Patients Bill of Rights" to give patients increased control over treatment options;
3. provide medical assistance and support to family caregivers who care for loved ones in the home; and
4. reimburse citizens who receive their health care through federally funded programs for emergency care treatment costs.

The president concluded that Congress' failure to reform health care ensures that delayed medical treatment will result in the denial of medical care.[23]

Finally, two days following the introduction of the Veteran's Millennium Health Care Act (VMHCA) of 1999, President William Jefferson Clinton addressed the nation on health care reform. In his weekly radio address, the president discussed legislative measures before Congress. He articulated support for legislative proposals that included:

1. a "Patients Bill of Rights"
2. reimbursement for emergency care treatment for individuals that receive their medical benefits through federally administered programs like Medicare, veteran's health care system and Medicaid
3. increased access to specialized medical treatment, i.e. chiropractic, mental health, etc.
4. managed care reform mechanisms
5. quality assurance mechanisms
6. increased access to specialized medical treatment, i.e. chiropractic, mental health, etc., and
7. expansion of preventative health care services.[24]

Communication with Interest Groups

Department of Veteran's Affairs and veteran's organizations were supportive of the Clinton's effort to increase access to health care services. In May 1993, the president thanked the veteran's community for supporting his health care reform plan. Clinton also thanked the Veteran's Administration for its work with the White House Task Force on health care reform.[25] In November of the same year, the president traveled to VA medical facilities throughout the United States garnering support for health care reform. While visiting medical facilities operated by the Department of Veteran's Affairs, President Clinton saluted veterans for their efforts to protect the United States. In acknowledging their sacrifices, Clinton stated that the country could never truly repay its debt to veterans. However, the president stressed that the government could show its gratitude for their service by ensuring that veterans have access to comprehensive health care services. He also spoke of legislation introduced by the Democratic Party to increase cost-of-living allowances (COLA) for disabled veterans. Furthermore, President Clinton highlighted his health care reform goals. Among the measures discussed were:

1. affordable health care;
2. quality health care for veterans;
3. comprehensive health care for veterans;
4. increased access to VA operated hospitals and health care facilities;
5. removing copayment or deductible requirements for low-income and disabled veterans whose injury was sustained during their military service; and
6. the expansion of long-term health care services for veterans;
7. the right of all veterans to have access to VA facilities and medical services.[26]

President Clinton made similar statements at Memorial Day celebrations. While attending a Veteran's Day Breakfast Celebration in 1993, the president spoke of his administration's commitment to health care, particularly veteran's health care issues. Furthermore, throughout his administration, he traveled the country making appealing to the public for improved veteran's benefits. During a celebration at Arlington Cemetery, President Clinton pushed for improvements in the "Montgomery GI Bill." He vowed that the veteran's education benefit would enable veterans to secure higher education. Clinton maintained that improvements in the education benefit would help revitalize the economy veterans are given additional life skills to help them reach their full potential.[27] He, further, highlighted the impact of the program on veterans. The president maintained that the "GI Bill" has helped more than 15 million veterans. He stressed many veterans flocked to colleges and trade schools throughout the country. Consequently, over 450,000 World War II veterans became engineers; 360,000 became teachers and 180,000 became health care professionals. Hence, President Clinton maintained that the "GI Bill" helped veterans achieve their piece of the American dream.[28]

Finally, President William Jefferson Clinton shared his views on the veteran's reform legislation with veterans during the Veterans of Foreign Wars (VFW) national convention. He told those in attendance he favored increasing the quality of medical services available in VA medical facilities. The president also stressed the need to expand health care coverage to Gulf War veterans who suffer from illnesses linked to their service in the Persian Gulf War. Furthermore, he indicated his support for outreach programs that help to eradicate homelessness in the veteran's community. The president declared, "they should be brought back into the society they did so much to defend."[29]

Moreover, President Clinton spoke of his intent to sign the Veteran's Millennium Health Care Act. During a Veteran's Day celebration, Clinton acknowledge his support for a number of the bills provisions that would:

1. increase the availability of burial space in VA cemeteries through use of flat grave markers;
2. Increase veteran's access to VA medical treatment centers;
3. Increase veteran's salaries, pensions and compensation;
4. increase outreach efforts to assist homeless veterans;
5. expand long-term health care services for disabled and elderly veterans;
6. reimburse veterans or private hospitals for emergency care services provided to veterans; and
7. increase access to nursing home care services.

President Clinton remarked that reforming these benefits and services would "help to redeem their sacrifice"[30] Clinton also vowed that America must repay its debt to veterans so that the problems that plagued veterans in the 20th century do not haunt them in the new millennium. Specifically, the president said that "by doing all we can to see that the horrors of the 20th century's wars are not visited upon the 21st century Americans."[31]

The Budget as a Tool of Influence

The president of the United States also the power to construct the federal budget. According to Larry Sabato in *Goodbye to Good-Time Charlie: The American Governor Transformed*, the authority to prepare the budget is the most important weapon or power an executive possesses in his or her dealings with Congress. He maintains that when the budget is utilized properly, it heavily reflects the president's political agenda. As such, the budget proposal prepared by the Chief Executive speaks volumes about the priorities of his administration. Furthermore, the budget proposed by the president offers the best statement reflects the realities of his administrative and programmatic goals.[32]

However, the president's power in this area does not go unchecked. Congress has the legal authority to modify the executive budget. Generally, Congress tends to make small changes rather than massive changes to the president's budget proposal. According to Nachos and Bump in their article "Policy and Priority in the Budgetary Process, claim that Congress only makes major changes in ten (10) percent of the items.

Although the budget-making authority of the president offers a broad base for him to wield power influence, it is his power to veto legislation, which is perhaps the most powerful. The power to veto legislative acts is yet another tool in the president's arsenal of weapons he can employ in his dealings with Congress. Ultimately, the authority to veto legislation is viewed, as the most powerful tool possessed by the Chief Executive in his attempt to influence Congress. Furthermore, in 1996, Congress passed legislation that empowered President Clinton to have line item veto authority over the federal budget. However, in *Clinton, President of the United States, et al. v. City of New York et al*, the Supreme Court struck down the Line Item Veto Act in 1998. It ruled that the law was unconstitutional because the president is required to either accept of reject legislation in its entirety. In his budgetary dealings with Congress, President William Jefferson Clinton used the line-item veto on eighty-two (82) occasions.[33] Nevertheless, Samuel B. Hoff in his paper on the pocket veto power of the president points to the president ability to prevent a bill from being enacted by not signing it. This authority is referred to as the pocket veto. This is an effective tool utilized when Congress has adjourned shortly after having sent the bill to the president for his consideration.[34]

The ability of the president to deliver messages to the legislature is another basis of influence on the legislative process. A skillful and perceptive executive can use this requirement to focus both legislative and public attention on his program. Throughout the nation's history, American presidents have made a point of uses messages to apply pressure and generate support for his program goals. While these messages may be informative, they are often filled with "civic platitudes" or symbolic gestures. However, on occasion the president offers a message for bold new programs. Furthermore, the influence a president experiences through use of public messages is determined by his perception of its value.[35]

President William Jefferson Clinton utilized a variety of tools and strategies to influence the enactment of the Veteran's Millennium Health Care Act (VMHCA) of 1999. The president used persuasion, negotiation, and compromise as tools of influencing Congress. President Clinton also communicated with interest groups like the American Legion and Veterans of Foreign Wars (VFW). He also articulated his support for the veteran's reform bill through use of his bureaucracy as a tool. In addition, the president made use of the media to carry his message to Congress and the American public.

Bureaucracy as a Means of Influence

The President of the United States has within his arsenal authority over the executive offices. As the Chief Executive, he is expected to manage a bureaucracy, oversee subordinates, and implement public policy.[36] However, the president has very little tangible authority to carry out such policies. He, therefore, relies on the expertise of civil servants to fulfill this responsibility. As such, the president delegates some of his authority to top executives within the various department and agencies under his charge. This remains a vital tool. Many departmental representatives and bureaucrats have maintained long-standing relationships with the national legislature. They also have a wealth of experience servicing clientele groups. In addition, government bureaucrats are responsible for establishing methods of operation. They often reflect ideological and professional biases. Consequently, depending on the department, the president may encounter a degree of resistance from bureaucrats and civil servants responsible for program implementation.[37] In the case of the Department of Veteran's Affairs, little resistance appears to have existed between the administration's policy objectives and those of bureaucrats.

The importance of civil servants rests in their expertise. They are responsible for interpreting the meaning of statutes and regulations. In fact, senior administrators make substantive policy decisions. The primary means by which the president directs the executive branch is through use of his authority to appoint high-ranking officials. Every Chief Executive seeks to appoint people who will be loyal to his administrative goals and objectives. Furthermore, appointees need to have a high degree of managerial experience. They must possess the ability to represent valuable political constituencies. In this instance, the primary political constituency that the Veteran's Administration represents is the veteran's community.[38] President Clinton appointed Togo West as Secretary of the Department of Veteran's Affairs. The president believed he had both the experience necessary and the ability to represent veterans. During Congress' consideration of the Veteran's Millennium Health Care Act, Stephen Backhus, Director of the Veteran's Affairs and Military Health Care Issues, and Kenneth Kizer, Undersecretary for Health were also responsible for making substantive contributions to the veteran's reform bill.

The primary means by which differences are resolved between the views of the Executive (Department of Veteran's Affairs) and Congress generally occurs in legislative hearings, oversight hearings, and mark-ups. These forums are used as a means to negotiate and compromise on policy decisions. The President is armed with departmental heads that articulate the administration's views and position on issues. As part of President Clinton's bureaucracy, the United States Under-Secretary for Health for the U.S. Department of Veteran's Affairs, Kenneth Kizer, and the Deputy Under-Secretary for Health, Thomas Garthwaite were instrumental in articulating the Clinton administration's policy preferences of veteran's benefits. Stephen Backhus, Director of Veteran's Affairs and Military Health Issues, also actively participated in the shaping and passage of the veteran's legislation. The three men testified at several congressional committee hearings. They testified at hearings before the Veteran's Affairs Committee, and its Subcommittee on Hospitals and Health. As such, key bureaucrats within the Department of Veteran's Affairs were given the opportunity to appear before the Veteran's Affairs Committee in the House of Representatives and Senate to discuss the Clinton administration's concerns regarding the implementation of veteran's health care. Congress also utilized hearings to determine how effectively the executive branch, in this case the Department of Veteran's Affairs, provides veteran's health care services. While it is sometimes difficult to control the actions of bureaucrats, William Brigman in his article "The Executive Branch and the Independent Regulatory Agencies," stresses that the Chief Executive has more influence over department, agencies and commissions than is typically assumed.[39]

Testimony of the Department of Veteran's Affairs

On March 10, 1999, the Subcommittee on Health held a hearing on the status of VA health care in the United States. On behalf of the administration, Stephen Backhus, Director of Veteran's Affairs and Military Health Care Issues appeared before Congress to discuss budgetary and infrastructure planning within the department. At the heart of his testimony was the administration's belief that the VA could no longer afford to spend one-fourth of its budget on maintaining outdated, underused or unused medical facilities. Backhus explained to members of the subcommittee that escalating costs in the health care profession were draining the Veteran's Administration's budget. He stated that the department expects to spend close to one-fourth of its budget during fiscal years 2000 through 2004 on operating; maintaining and renovating VA owned facilities. Backhus asserted that additional funding is necessary in order for the administration to effectively implement the veteran's health care system. In fact, he argued that the Department of Veteran's Affairs needed an additional $20 billion to sustain its old infrastructure from 2000 through 2004. He also maintained that the VA failed to compare "life-cycle costs" and other alternative methods to identify ways in which the needs of America's veterans can be met in a manner that reduces VA expenditures. The department has been confronted with two competing ideals - meeting veteran's medical needs and cutting the department's overhead costs for maintaining veteran's health care. The Department of Veteran's Affairs also requested that legislative action be taken to assist the VA to increase financial savings by removing mandates that require the VA to maintain and operate old and obsolete facilities that are either underused or vacant. The department argued that it should be allowed to sell, lease, or demolish outdated and unused buildings.[40]

Furthermore, Backhus emphasized fiscal constraints involved in constructing new facilities forced the veteran's administration to divide its 181 delivery sites into 22 geographic regions. Such geographic divisions would be better served with the limited resources. Each geographic region has between 6 and 12 major delivery locations. These regions are referred to as Veteran's Integrated Service Networks (VISN). Each network has a regional director and a small staff that is responsible for carrying out a broad scope of activities including budgeting, asset, and infrastructure planning. However, Backhus recommended to Congress that the budget appropriations of the departments should be increased by $20 billion in order for the department to continue maintaining its currently owned or leased medical facilities. He asserted that the increase in the budgetary appropriation is necessary to meet up with the anticipated operations and maintenance costs, which the department is likely to incur over the next five years. When questioned about why such a major portion of the VA's budget (close to $4 billion) was authorized to maintaining and operating facilities, Backhus explained that the amount spent was based on such factors such as underused property, the age of buildings owned by the Veteran's Health Administration, and less than one-fourth of the 1,200 buildings are used to deliver services to veterans.[41]

In the case of maintaining old buildings, Backhus explained that approximately one-third of the buildings owned by the department are historically significant based on the age of the building and the architectural and history of the site. The majority of the buildings are listed with the National Register of Historic Places and as such are protected under the law that governs historic sites. Therefore, the Veteran's Administration is required by the law to comply with special procedures for maintaining and disposing of buildings. He informed Congress that 181 major veteran's locations have historic buildings located within their infrastructure. Only one-fourth or 1,200 buildings out of approximately 4,800 are used to deliver health care services to veterans. The remaining buildings are primarily used to support health care activities. Backhus stated that the Veteran's Administration has over 5 million square feet of vacant space that costs the department approximately 35 million a year to maintain.[42]

Backhus suggested that the administration should be allowed to reduce the level of funding spent on old, underused, inefficient or obsolete buildings because the costs associated with operating and maintaining VA facilities are extremely high. The administration argued that if Congress allowed the department to reduce funding for maintaining or renovating old and outdated facilities, the Veteran's Administration could provide medical services more efficiently by investing the savings in facilities that exist in locations where there are large concentrations of veterans.[43]

Assistant Secretary Backhus suggested that the VA's best opportunity to accumulate financial resources for infrastructure improvements could come from operational savings if the department is allowed to restructure its current capital improvement system. He argued that legislation "could authorize the VHA to deposit the savings into a capital asset fund . . . which might save $180 million a year."[44] As such, the administration argued that if, for example, the health administration is permitted to develop a means by which veterans needs can be met with one less facility in one of the nine major multiple locations; savings could in turn be used to acquire new buildings in the future. Finally, the veteran's health administration requested that legislative action be taken that would authorize the VA to accumulate funds in its Capital Asset Fund by charging delivery locations for costs associated with building renovations or acquiring new buildings. Backhus argued that the administration could then utilize returns on capital investments such as operational savings or payments made by third parties for a veteran's medical treatment.[45]

Although the Veteran's Administration acknowledges several weaknesses in the delivery of veteran's health care services, the administration maintained that with the proper legislative relief the department could cut its expenditures related to maintaining buildings.[46]

In addition, Thomas L. Garthwaite, M.D., Deputy Under-Secretary for Health at the Department of Veteran's Affairs, appeared before the Veteran Affairs Committee's Subcommittee on Health to discuss the Veteran's Health Administration's planning, budgeting and management of capital assets. Dr. Garthwaite began his testimony by acknowledging that the department was plagued with serious managerial and operational problems in the early 1990's. However, he noted that since 1995 the VA has made progress in transitioning from a disease-oriented, hospital based system to that of a more patient oriented focusing on preventative health care and community-based facilities. He stated that the department shifted its focus from primary servicing veterans suffering from chronic illnesses to primary care services. Although the VA is in the midst of transforming the health care system, Garthwaite highlighted several departmental accomplishments. He stressed the departments shift from in-patient care services to out-patient services reduced the number of hospital care beds by 52 percent between fiscal year 1994 and 1999. Furthermore, he stressed that the number of in-patient admissions declined by 32 percent since 1994. He testified that the VA was in the process of merging 48 hospitals or clinic systems into 23 local integrated health care systems. Additionally, he maintained that the Department of Veteran's Affairs had sited 271 new community-based outpatient clinics since 1995. Garthwaite stressed that these changes occurred largely due to rapid changes in health care technology. In fact, such rapid change, he stated, makes it difficult for the Veteran's Administration to develop capital asset plans.[47]

Thomas Garthwaite maintained that the Veteran's Health Administration's budget proposal for fiscal year 2000 recommended that Congress fund three major construction projects be funded in order to improve VA operated facilities. Among the recommendations was a project for a spinal cord injury facility in Tampa, Florida and a new surgical suite to be located in Kansas City, Missouri. Additionally, the Department of Veteran's Affairs proposed that psychiatric nursing units be renovated in Murfreesboro, Tennessee. Finally, the VA suggested that 39 buildings at a medical center in Leavenworth, Kansas be demolished because they were no longer needed to expand the National Cemetery in the area. Garthwaite urged the subcommittee to fund the department's authorization request for the above-mentioned medical projects.[48] In addition, Deputy-Secretary Garthwaite discussed the department's initiative to increase flexibility through a pilot program that would improve the management of its infrastructure by encouraging and streamlining the process of converting properties no longer needed or used by the department into assets. He added that the proposal would allow the department to dispose of underutilized or unused buildings, land, or equipment by selling, transferring, or exchanging the property. Placing all proceeds into a Capital Asset Fund could reinvest the resulting saving earmarked in this plan. He suggested the establishment of this fund in order to ensure that the VA has a means to become less financially dependent on Congress for funding. Lastly, he suggested that a cap of $50 million be placed on the amount allowed to accumulate in the fund. He maintained that any additional funds should be transferred into the department's minor construction program.[49]

Garthwaite also proposed that the VA support homeless veterans by directing at least 10 percent of proceeds from disposal and the sale of underused or old buildings, land, and equipment to local homeless assistance groups, which would include support for veterans. Additionally, he stated that the department would use an additional 5 percent of its proceeds from the sale of old property to support homeless programs that specifically served the veteran's population.[50]

Following the oversight hearings on the status of the VA health care delivery system, Representative Cliff Stearns (R-FL) drafted the Veteran's Millennium Health Care Act aimed increasing access to long-term care and creating additional means by which the VA could become less dependent on federal funds to sustain veteran's services. During the first mark-up on the Veteran's Millennium Health Care Act held on May 19, 1999, the Director of Veteran's Affairs and Military Health Issues, Stephen Backhus, expressed the administration's support for and reservations about several aspects of the bill. Stephen Backhus, Director of Veteran's Affairs and Military Health Care Issues, appeared before the House Veteran's Affairs' Subcommittee on Health to discuss various aspects of the "draft" proposal of the Veteran's Millennium Health Care Act. He noted that the increase in federal mandates placed a series of burdens on the VA, which limits its ability to effectively administer the veteran's health care system. Additionally, Backhus maintained that many of the mandates were unnecessary because the department had taken the initiative in October 1995 to transform its health care delivery system from operating in-patient hospitals to the utilization of regional networks. He explained that the department had begun to use non-VA health care providers in an effort to provide services to veterans in a more efficient and effective manner. He made note of the fact that following the passage of the "Veteran's Health Care Eligibility Reform Act of 1996", the VA was required to enroll veterans for health care coverage based on priority groups. Backhus argued that the department complied with the federal mandate as best as it could within its limited resources. He continued that in January of 1997, in response to this mandate, the Veteran's Administration proposed a five-year spending plan in an effort to reduce per-patient costs by approximately 30 percent. Furthermore, he stated that the Department of Veteran's Affairs increased the number of veterans served through the health care system by 20 percent. Additionally, Backhus pointed to the fact that the VA reduced its reliance on congressional budget appropriations by 10 percent.[51]

Stephen Backhus discussed the fact that on numerous occasions the department had presented reports and testified before the Subcommittee on Health on the VA's ongoing attempts to transform the health care delivery system. Backhus' testimony on May 19, 1999 focused on three primary areas of concern: (1) access to long-term health care services; (2) the realignment of services at old and underused medical facilities and (3) revenue sharing for medical care. Backhus maintained that the proposed bill would in fact facilitate the Veteran's Administration's ongoing transformation of its health care delivery system as well as address budgetary issues previously reported to Congress by the Department of Veteran's Affairs. Additionally, he asserted that the proposals included in the Act would assist the department in creating a framework that would address the increasing health needs of the aging population of veterans within the available resources.[52]

Again, Stephen Backhus emphasized the VA's extensive and aging infrastructure. The administration requested that Congress allow it to realign facilities. He avowed that by permitting the VA to realign its facilities, the Department of Veteran's Affairs could better identify unnecessary delivery locations and redirects the maintenance and operation budgets from areas with underused buildings. Backhus also noted that if the VA were not authorized to realign its health care delivery system, operating and maintenance costs would continue to increase and create less access to veterans services.[53]

On the other hand, Backhus argued that the VA faces major challenges in providing services to a rapidly aging veteran population. He pointed out that 34 percent of the veteran's population in the United States is 65 and older. Consequently, he maintained that as of 1999, the Department of Veteran's Affairs expects to spend $2 billion of its $18.4 billion health care budget on providing long-term health care services to eligible veterans. Of the $2 billion spent on long-term care, $1.7 billion was spent on 131 VA operated nursing homes, contracts with nursing facilities and state veteran's homes. He noted that the remaining $353 million is spent on non-institutional alternatives such as residential care, adult day care, respite care and home care services.[54] However, the Department of Veteran's Affairs declared that while the legislation would assist the VA in improving its health care delivery system, the bill created major challenges for the Department of Veteran's Affairs. More specifically, Backhus maintained that the bill should help the VA provide services to veterans in more appropriate settings and reduce patient costs. This will further increase the number of patients. He testified that the legislation would also reduce the VA's dependence on budget appropriations by allowing the department to invest funds in a Capital Investment Fund. The fund will allow the department to acquire new facilities in a more expedient manner by allowing the VA to accumulate asset capital. He recognized that long-term care provisions included in the bill were designed in a manner that should reduce variability in veteran's access to medical services nationwide. Finally, he pointed to the fact that the bill allows veterans to make additional demands for VA health care services. This is largely due to increased numbers of veterans would utilize the VA's outpatient services. Because of increased demands for services, Backhus directed the subcommittee's attention to the Congressional Budget Office's report, which estimated that increased use of the health care system could increase program expenditures by billions of dollars. [55]

On the other hand, Stephen Backhus asserted that the "draft" bill would require the VA to incorporate into its health care benefits package additional long-term care categories for services. Stephen Backhus noted concern that should the long-term care mandate require an expansion in services, the department would only be able to provide such service to eligible veterans when resources are available.[56]

Backhus contended that the legislation would affect the Veteran's Administration's ongoing transformation. He maintained that although the administration has taken efforts to reform many aspects of the Veteran's Administration. He stated that despite the fact that the bill provided a "rational framework" for the manner in which the VA should function, additional resources would be necessary in order for the Department of Veteran's Affairs to implement the proposed measures. He explained that the department was forced to operate with limited financial resources.[57] Backhus, however, acknowledged that the legislation would assist the Veteran's Administration to "provide care for veterans in more appropriate settings . . ."[58] Furthermore, he submitted that the long-term health care provisions in the legislation were designed in a manner that would reduce variances in access to health care system. He highlighted the fact that decaying medical infrastructure was in need of enhancement.

In fact, he argued that the greatest obstacle facing the Department of Veteran's Affairs was that of old and obsoletes medical facilities.[59]

The Director perorated that while the legislation would enable the Department of Veteran's Affairs to achieve its goals of providing improved long-term care, facility service realignment, and cost sharing, the legislation had far reaching implications for the administration. For example, he stated that the bill would result in changes that would assist the Veteran's Administration in appropriate settings while simultaneously reducing the department's reliance on federally appropriated funds. Furthermore, Backhus contended that facility realignment and cost sharing provisions in the bill were consistent with options the administration suggested in previous hearings as a means to reducing budgetary pressures and generating additional resources for the department. He suggested that part of the problem the VA faces is the result of a decision to focus on utilizing technological advances and medical specialization instead of providing hospital care to veterans. Consequently, the health care system was outpaced by societal changes, which necessitated a shift in policy towards managed care.[60]

In addition, the Director asserted that while the legislation enhanced long-term care services available to veterans, the Veteran's Administration (VA) would continue to face major challenges in serving an aging population of veterans. He maintained that approximately 34 percent of the veteran population is 65 or older. Thus, the aging veteran's population was likely to result in an increase need for long-term care services. Backhus noted that there were approximately 4 million veterans enrolled in the Veteran's Administration's (VA's) health care system. He explained that the VA provided health care services to an average of 63,000 veterans per day.[61]

Nevertheless, Backhus asserted that the administration was pleased with three features which will assist the VA in enhancing veteran's access to long-term care services: (1) the Act requires the development of a national program of long-term health care services; (2) mandates that the VA cover long-term care services for specified high-priority veterans such as those having received the Purple Heart and (3) increases the percentage of the Veteran's Administration's budget to be spent on non-institutional long-term care alternatives. In addition, the veteran's administration expressed its satisfaction that Congress gave the VA the flexibility to develop and structure long-term care services. He also applauded the attempt by Congress to improve access to long-term care services for the aging population of veterans in America. Additionally, he noted that the Act gave the Department of Veteran's Affairs the flexibility to generate additional revenue in the form of increasing copayments charged to veterans. The ability to increase the copayment scale would allow the VA to offset budget constraints as well as increase veteran's access to health care services provided by the Department of Veteran's Affairs. Lastly, Backhus stated that the Veteran's Millennium Health Care Act (VMHCA) of 1999 was a bill that, if enacted in to law, would allow the VA to improve on the quality of health care in a manner that would be "consistent with the overall goal of the VA's enrollment process."[62]

In addition, Kenneth W. Kizer, Under Secretary for Health for the Department of Veteran's Affairs also testified before the House Veteran's Affairs Committee's Subcommittee on Health and succinctly addressed the provisions of the draft bill on May 19, 1999. He acknowledged that the bill would require the department to develop and implement a plan to increase the options and services available for home care by January 1, 2000. He added that the legislation would require the Veteran's Administration to increase the percentage of its medical care budget for long-term care services. Furthermore, he continued that the Act mandates that the administration ensure that national staffing levels remain equal to that of fiscal year 1998. The draft bill would also require the Secretary of the Department of Veteran's Affairs to increase the availability of extended or long-term care services to veterans. Kizer expressed the VA's opposition to the provisions, which placed mandates on staffing levels. He asserted that it was unnecessary to mandate an additional planning process because the VA is committed to increasing home and community-based care funding levels in the budget for fiscal year 2000. He noted that the Department of Veteran's Affairs intend to continue with its efforts to shift financial resources to long-term care services and programs that increase veteran's access to such services.[63]

He discussed the provision in the bill that would create a new group eligible for priority care - veterans who were "injured in combat." He pointed out the vagueness of the language and concerns about the operational definition of the phrase "injured in combat." This group would be given the same priority or consideration as former prisoners of war (POW's) and veterans suffering with "service-connected" injuries rated by the VA as 10 to 20 percent. He articulated the department's general support for the provision, but urged Congress to be mindful that little data exists on the number of veterans that fall into this category. Subsequently, the language was modified and "injured in combat" was defined as veterans who received the Purple Heart Award.[64]

Kenneth Kizer expressed departmental support for the "co-payment" provision that modifies the law to give the Secretary of the Department of Veteran's Affairs flexibility to increase the co-payment that would be required of veterans who receive outpatient treatment. He stated that veterans were required to pay 20 percent of the average cost of an outpatient visit. As such, Kizer expressed the department's support for increased flexibility in developing copayments charged to veterans for medical treatment. He maintained that the Department of Veteran's Affairs embraces the change because it will allow the department to impose copayments that are consistent with health care industry "copayment" norms. He argued that any increased revenue received from copayments for hearing aids and electronic equipment could be deposited in a new Health Services Improvement Fund. The new fund is established by Congress as an account to which funds received or collected in the form of pharmacy copayments, medical equipment such a hearing aids and resources generated from entering into lease agreement for medical treatment space. Furthermore, any funds recovered from TRICARE, the Department of Defense's (DOD) health care program, could be deposited in the fund. Under the Act, the DOD is required to reimburse the Department of Veteran's Affairs for medical treatment provided to military retirees who are eligible for health care in VA facilities. The revenue deposited in the fund, he argues, could then be utilized to provide additional health care services to veterans. Under Secretary Kizer expressed support for TRICARE reimbursement and stated the provision would allow the Secretary of the Department of Veteran's Affairs greater flexibility in creating co-payments for services and equipment such as hearing aids, eyeglasses and medical equipment not related to veteran military service.[65]

Additionally, the VA supported provisions in the Act that mandated the extension of adult day health care services to veterans enrolled in the VA health care system. This provision covers veterans who would otherwise be forced to reside in a nursing home. He also noted that the legislation allows the Department of Veteran's Affairs to provide respite care to veterans in VA facilities. Furthermore, respite services are to be made available to the spouse or family who cares for the veterans in his or her home environment. The bill authorizes the

Veterans Administration to pay a "per diem" to State operated nursing homes for all of extended care services. The VA supported the provision because it would give the administration and states increased flexibility to collaborate different avenues to provide increased access to long-term care services. While Kizer expressed the administration's support for extended care services being included in the Act, he expressed concern about cost issues.[66]

Moreover, Under Secretary Kizer favored the establishment of a Veteran's Tobacco Trust Fund claiming that it would create another fund to which funds or proceeds received from government driven litigation against tobacco manufacturers could be deposited. He argued that the fund could in turn be used to conduct research related to tobacco addition in veterans, as well as for the development of prevention and treatment of illnesses associated with tobacco such as cancer.[67]

The Department of Veteran's Affairs stressed its support for provisions in the bill that is designed to increase veteran's access to and receipt of quality treatment. Kizer argued that the bill could give the Secretary the authority to contract medical services for veterans enrolled in the program. In addition, the Act would also authorize the department to lease property or equipment that is under utilized or unused to provide other forms of care to the veterans (e.g., outpatient care, nursing home care and long-term institutional care).[68]

Kizer also supported the provision in the bill that allowed veterans to participate in the development of network strategic planning requirements. The provision created a means by which veterans could share their views with administrators and have those views and or opinions possibly incorporated into the creation of strategic planning objectives. Furthermore, Under Secretary Kizer noted that this mandate required the Department of Veteran's Affairs to submit each plan to the congressional committees with jurisdiction. However, he expressed opposition to the requirement that prohibits the VA from implementing any plans for 45 days during a session of Congress.[69]

The draft Veteran's Millennium Health Care Act also included several provisions that would extend existing committee, reporting and program responsibilities. The draft proposed extending the department's authority to provide mental health care in the form of counseling to Vietnam veterans who served during the war in hostile areas after May 7, 1975. The measure extended the viability of readjustment counseling from 1999 through 2002. Under Secretary

Kizer noted the department's satisfaction with the extension of the mental health component for Vietnam veterans because the program was scheduled to expire on January 1, 2000. In addition, the draft bill proposed extending a requirement which mandated the Secretary of the Department of Veteran's Affairs to submit updated reports and comments to congressmen planning strategies, activities and recommendations made by the department's Committee on the Care of Severely, Chronically Mentally Ill Veterans. The VA agreed to provide annual reports to Congress on the department's ability to meet the treatment and rehabilitation needs of "severely, chronically ill veterans."[70] He voiced his satisfaction for the renewal of the requirement that called on the Secretary of the Department of Veteran's Affairs to submit a report to the House and Senate Committees on Veteran's Affairs on special programs utilized by the department to diagnose and treat veterans suffering with Post-Traumatic Stress Disorder (PTSD). This requirement compelled the department to reestablish its special Committee on Post-Traumatic Disorder. However, Kizer maintained that a better alternative exists. He suggested that the department be authorized to establish a working group on Post-Traumatic Stress Disorder. The working group, he maintained, could be a subcommittee of the already existing Committee on the Care of Severely, Chronically Mentally Ill Veterans. The Under Secretary for Health asserted that the creation of a working group would preserve the committee's role of advising the Veteran's Administration and Congress on the VA's capacity and effectiveness associated with implementing the mental health component of the health care system.[71] In addition, Under Secretary for Health Kenneth Kizer echoed the VA's support for extending its Homeless Providers Grant and Per Diem Program through September 30, 2002. He declared that in its last five rounds of funding, the VA received more than 600 grant applications requesting a total of $150 million for renovation and construction efforts that were designed to create supportive housing and service facilities for homeless veterans. Included in the proposals were requests for funding to acquire transport vans that would be used to increase program outreach to homeless veterans. He stated that there were 30 programs, which provided housing or homeless shelters for veterans. Furthermore, he asserted that more than 2,580 veterans received services from community based programs and residential care for veterans was provided for a total of 208,102 days. Finally, Kizer supported a provision in the Act that would remove the restriction previously placed on the number of grants the VA could award to programs for the procurement of transport vans. The previous law limited the Department of Veteran's Affairs to award only 20 grants to programs wishing to acquire transportation for homeless outreach programs. Therefore, he offered the administration's support for the provision due to the need for increased outreach to homeless veterans.[72]

The Under Secretary for Health for the Department of Veteran's Affairs remarked that the legislation proposed that the VA establish three pilot programs; the administration favored the creation of a program that would assist veterans with assisted living services. He also expressed the department's support for a pilot program that is designed to provide services to dependents of veterans. He argued that such a program would allow eligible dependents of veterans enrolled in the VA health care system to receive medical treatment from the Veteran's Administration. He explained that such services could be provided directly by the VA or through contractual agreements with non-VA facilities. "Eligible Dependents" are defined as those dependents that are either a spouse or child of a veteran enrolled in the VA health care system. He asserted that the department would agree to provide medical care to dependents of veterans on the condition that those services do not interfere with the availability of veteran's services. However, Kizer cautioned that dependents must agree to pay copayments and must provide health care insurance information to the VA. Furthermore, he stressed the fact that dependents should be required to release of medical records, information, and insurance information that the VA could use in seeking reimbursement medical services.[73]

Despite the Department of Veteran's Affairs cooperation with the legislative process in coining a new law, the Department opposed the establishment of a demonstration program to evaluate the need for chiropractic treatment by veterans. The Act authorizes the program to be established in as many as five medical treatment facilities. The establishment of such a program would allow the Veteran's Administration to hire and contract with chiropractors or chiropractic treatment facilities for the duration of the program. Congress stipulated that the pilot program could operate from October 1, 2000 to September 2001. Kizer maintained that the VA opposed the provision because it created additional paperwork by requiring the VA to submit a report to Congress before July 1, 2000 on plans to implement the chiropractic pilot program. He also explained that the VA opposed the establishment of a chiropractic care pilot program because it currently hires or contracts chiropractic services.[74]

Lastly, Under Secretary Kenneth Kizer supported the emergency care provision in the Veteran's Millennium Health Care Act during the mark-up session held on May 19, 1999. He explained to members of the Subcommittee that the VA favored reimbursement veterans enrolled in the VA health care system for emergency treatment provided at non-VA treatment facilities. He favored the limit placed on eligibility for emergency services as long as the veterans had previously received medical treatment at VA facilities within the 12 months before the emergency. Although, Kizer expressed support the provision, he made it clear that he believed that the VA should only pay as a last resort. As such, Kenneth Kizer stressed that the VA would reimburse non-VA health care providers "only" when veterans lack medical coverage. Kizer stressed, in situations where veterans have insurance, the department's belief that the veteran's health care program would not provide reimbursement. Finally, the Under Secretary supported the measure because it helps the VA expand its ability to provide out-of network emergency care to veterans who lack priority status based on the type of injury sustained.[75]

Additionally, the administration opposed a provision that would limit the department's ability to close more than half of the beds or space. The VA, further, viewed the mandate of quarterly reporting requirement of any facility changes as burdensome on the agency. Under Secretary for Health, Kizer stated that the provision focuses on existing facilities as opposed to the ability of the VA to provide quality health care services. Furthermore, he maintained that the requirement is not cost-effective for the department because it required them to sustain space regardless of its utilization. In addition, Kizer noted that the provision decreased the VA flexibility to manage space or beds in facilities operated by the department. He asserted that the provision would cause a further delay in the administration's ability to act to improve the effectiveness of the VA health care system. Lastly, he argued the provision fails to allow the Department of Veteran's Affairs to decrease unnecessary spending.[76]

During the 2000 American presidential campaign year, democratic presidential nominee, Vice-President Albert Gore, announced in a speech before a group of veterans that "the Clinton administration will support a $1 billion increase in funding for veteran's health care services" for fiscal year 2001. However, the Joint Veteran's Affairs Committee in Congress recommended that the VA budget be increased by $1.7 billion. In response to Vice- President Gore's announcement, Butch Miller, national commander for the American Legion, praised the Clinton administration's support for increasing the VA budget as recognition of the diminishing quality of health care provided to veterans. However, he declared that the executive budget request falls short of what veteran's organizations, such as The American Legion, argue is necessary for the agency to "break even." The fiscal year 2001 budget request submitted by four veterans' organizations indicates that the VA budget needs to be increased by $3 billion in order to sustain the present level of services that they provide.[77]

At a signing ceremony of the Veteran's Millennium Health Care Act, President William Jefferson Clinton noted that the comprehensive bi-partisan bill would improve a large number of services and benefits provided to veterans by the Veterans Administration. In fact, President Clinton stressed that the Act is significant because the law offers veterans increased access to facilities administered by the Department of Veteran's Affairs. He added that the law would also expand the eligibility of veterans to available medical resources and it would authorize the Department of Veteran's Affairs to revise co-payments that are charged for some medical benefits such as hearing aids and prescription drugs. The President noted that the new law makes it easier for a surviving spouse of a disabled prisoner of war to qualify for benefits and services. Finally, the president expressed his appreciation to everyone involved in the formulation and passage of the comprehensive veteran's bill.[78]

Following the enactment of the new law, William Cohen, Secretary of Department of Defense (DOD), vowed to fight for increased budget appropriations for America's veterans. The Secretary argued that the government would not settle lawsuits charging that the government had reneged on its "promise" to veterans. However, Secretary Cohen stated "providing lifelong health care that older veterans were promised if they made military service a career is a "moral obligation" that the Pentagon will help fulfill.[79] Cohen maintained that the displeasure expressed by military retirees on health care benefits have negatively influenced recruitment efforts. He also told military retirees that the Clinton administration was working with

Congress to secure funding to increase veterans access to VA and Department of Defense health care systems.[80]

Conclusion

The Executive branch's influence in reforming and overhauling aspects of the Veteran's Millennium Health Care Act passed during the 106th Congress cannot be understated. Indeed, President Clinton and high-ranking bureaucrats in the Department of Veteran's Affairs played a critical role in shaping the comprehensive veteran's bill. Department of Veteran's Affairs' Under Secretary, Kenneth Kizer, and Director of Military Health Care Issues, Stephen Backhus, and Deputy Under Secretary Garthwaite, M.D. worked diligently to ensure that Congress did not pass additional mandates that would undermine the administration's efforts to effectively provide health care services to veterans. The Department of Veteran's Affairs supported many of the provisions in House bill H.R. 2116 - the Veteran's Millennium Health Care Act. Among those supported by the Clinton administration were:

1. Increasing access to veteran's health care facilities;
2. expanding long-term health care services for disabled veterans with "service-connected disabilities;
3. guaranteeing priority status to veterans who received a Purple Heart for courageous military service;
4. guaranteeing priority status to Prisoners of War (POWs);
5. increasing efforts to assist homeless veterans; and
6. reimbursing non-VA hospitals and medical personnel for emergency treatment provided to veterans enrolled in the VA health care system.

Conversely, the administration expressed its opposition to a number of the proposed provisions. The President opposed the congressional mandate to increase the number of options and services available for adult day health care services due to his belief that it would place an excessive burden on the veteran's administration. Secondly, while the president favored allowing veterans to receive care from specialists, i.e., cardiologists, mental health care professionals, chiropractic physicians, etc., the Department of Veteran's Affairs opposed the creation of a pilot program for chiropractic services. The administration also opposed reducing the number of outpatient facilities by an additional 50 percent. President Clinton argued that veterans needed increased access to inpatient facilities. His administration disagreed with the Department of Veteran's Affairs, which maintained that it is more cost-effective for veterans to receive outpatient care. This is largely because it costs an enormous amount to house patient in medical facilities than it does to allow them to recuperate at home. Finally, President Clinton disagreed with Congress' recommendation to increase the VA budget for fiscal year 2001 by $1.7 billion. The administration believed the requested increase was excessive. However, the president did favor increasing the VA budget by for $1 billion.

Although the Clinton administration vowed that veterans were entitled to improved access to quality health care services, its support was restricted by fiscal constraints on federal spending. The president supported increasing the VA budget for fiscal year 2001. However, the administration supported increasing the budget to the extent that other federal programs would experience a reduction in program funding. This is evident by the fact both the President's and Congress' recommended spending increases that were more than $2 billion less that the budget request submitted by the of veteran's organizations like the American Legion and Veterans of Foreign Wars.

Nevertheless, the final document signed into law by President William Jefferson Clinton was a "bi-partisan" bill. The president praised Congress for its concerted effort to eradicate problems associated with the delivery of veteran's health care and benefits programs. In addition, Clinton asserted that the bill represented the first comprehensive approach to redressing veterans concerns. He maintained that the new law would have a far-reaching impact of the delivery of veteran's benefits administered by the Department of Veteran's Affairs.

Notes

[1] *U.S. Constitution*, Article I, section 7.

[2] *U.S. Constitution*, Article II, section 3.

[3] Richard Neustadt, *Presidential Power* (New York: John Wiley and Sons, Inc., 1964), George Edwards, *Presidential Influence in Congress* (San Francisco:

W.H. Freeman and Company, 1980) and Clinton Rossiter, *The President. Office and Powers, 1787-1948 (New York: New York University Press (1948).*

[4] John Hart, "Congressional Reaction to the White House," Presidential Studies Quarterly, Vol. XI (Winter 1980), 83-91.

[5] George Edwards. *Presidential Influence in Congress* (San Francisco: W.H. Freeman and Company, 1980), 122.

[6] Ibid., 124-126.

[7] Ibid., 128.

[8] Ibid., 130-132.

[9] Ibid., 132-133.

[10] Ibid., 133.

[11] Ibid., 139-143.

[12] Ibid., 144.

[13] Richard Neustadt, "Presidency and Legislation: Planning the President's Program," in *The Presidency*, ed. Aaron Wildavsky (Boston: Little Brown, 1969), 596.

[14] George Edwards, *Presidential Influence in Congress* (San Francisco: W.H. Freeman, 1980), 128.

[15] William A. Reynolds, "Health Care reform: How Bright Prospects Plummeted," The *American College of Physicians Observer* (May 1997) [on-line journal} available from http://www.acponline.org/journals/news/may97/plummet.htm; Internet; accessed 19 September 2001, 2.

[16] Ibid.

[17] Mark V. Pauly, "Universal Health Insurance in the Clinton Plan: Coverage as a Tax-Financed Public Good," *Journal of Economic Perspectives* (Summer 1994), 46-47.

---

[18] U.S. President, *Public Papers of the Presidents of the United States* (Washington, D.C.: Office of the Federal Register, National Archives and Records Service, 1999), William Jefferson Clinton, 1999, 63.

[19] Ibid.

[20] Ibid.

[21] Ibid., 65.

[22] Ibid., 66.

[23] U.S. President, *Public Papers of the Presidents of the United States* (Washington, D.C.: Office of the Federal Register, National Archives and Records Service, 1999), William Jefferson Clinton, 1999, 201-205.

[24] U.S. President, *Public Papers of the Presidents of the United States* (Washington, D.C.: Office of the Federal Register, National Archives and Records Service, 1999), William Jefferson Clinton, 1999, 930.

[25] President William Clinton, "Remarks on the Observance of the 50th Anniversary of World War II", *Public Papers of Presidents*, vol. 1 (Washington, D.C: Government Printing Office, 1993), 783.

[26] U.S. President, *Public Papers of the Presidents of the United States* (Washington, D.C.: Office of the Federal Register, National Archives and Records Service, 1993), William Jefferson Clinton, 1993, 1956-1957.

[27] U.S. President, *Public Papers of the Presidents of the United States* (Washington, D.C.: Office of the Federal Register, National Archives and Records Service, 1993), William Jefferson Clinton, 1993, 1006.

[28] Ibid.

[29] U.S. President, *Public Papers of the Presidents of the United States* (Washington, D.C.: Office of the Federal Register, National Archives and Records Service, 1993), William Jefferson Clinton, 1999, 1446.

[30] Ibid., 2074

[31] Ibid.

[32] Larry Sabato, *Goodbye to Good-Time Charlie: The American Governor Transformed,* 2nd ed. (Washington, D.C.: Congressional Quarterly Press, 1983), 83.

---

[33] *Clinton, President of the United States, et al. v. City of New York et al, [66 U.S.L.W. 4543]*. Robert Spitzer provides a discussion of the line-item veto conflict in "The Item Veto Dispute and Secular Crisis of the Presidency," *Presidential Studies Quarterly,* vol. XXVIII (Fall 1998), 799-815.

[34] Samuel Hoff, "The Presidential Pocket Veto: Its Use and Legality," *Journal of Policy History*, vol. VI (n.d. 1994), 188-208.

[35] William O'Keefe and Morris Ogul, *The American Legislative Process*, 10th ed., (New Jersey: Prentice Hall, 2001), 399.

[36] Raymond Tatalovich and Byron Daynes, *Presidential Power in the United States* (Belmont, California: Brooks Cole Publishing Company, 1984), 191.

[37] Ibid., 208.

[38] Ibid., 193.

[39] William Brigman, "The Executive Branch and the Independent Regulatory Agencies," *Presidential Studies Quarterly* (Spring 1981), 244-246.

[40] U.S. Congress, Committee on Veteran's Affairs, Subcommittee on Hospitals and Health, *VA Health Care: Planning, Budgeting and Management of Capital Assets,* report by Stephen Backhus, 106th Cong., 1st sess., 1999 [database on-line] available from http://veterans.house.gov/hearings/schedule106/mar99/3-10-99HEA/gao.htm; Internet; accessed 5 February 2000, 1-2.

[41] Ibid., 3-6.

[42] Ibid., 3-5.

[43] Ibid., 1-2.

[44] Ibid.

[45] Ibid, 11-12.

[46] Ibid., 12.

[47] U.S. Congress, Committee on Veteran's Affairs, Subcommittee on Hospitals and Health, *VA Health Care: Planning, Budgeting and Management of Capital Assets,* report by Thomas Garthwaite, 106th Cong., 1st sess., 1999 [database on-

line] available from http://veterans.house.gov/hearings/schedule106/mar99/3-10-99HEA/gao.htm; Internet; accessed 5 February 2000, 1-2.

48 Ibid., 3-4.

49 Ibid., 4-5.

50 Ibid.,5.

51 U.S. Congress, House, Committee on Veteran's Affairs, Subcommittee on Hospitals and Health, *The Veteran's Millennium Health Care Act*, H.R. 2116, report by Stephen Backhus, 106th Congress, 1st sess., [database on-line] available from http://veterans.house.gov/hearings/schedule106/may99/5-19-99HEA/gao.htm; Internet; accessed 5 February 2000, 1-3.

52 Ibid.

53 Ibid., 6-7.

54 Ibid., 9-10.

55 Ibid., 3-5.

56 Ibid., 10.

57 Ibid.1-3.

58 Ibid.

59 Ibid.

60 Ibid., 3-4.

62 Ibid., 10-19.

63 U.S. Congress, House, Committee on Veteran's Affairs, Subcommittee on Hospitals and Health, *The Proposed Veteran's Millennium Health Care Act*, report by Kenneth Kizer, 106th Cong., 1st sess., 1999 [database on-line] available from http://veterans.house.gov/hearings/schedule106/may99/5-19-99HEA/gao.htm; Internet; accessed 5 February 2000, 3-4.

64 Ibid., 5.

65 Ibid., 5-8.

[66] Ibid., 4.

[67] Ibid., 8-9.

[68] Ibid., 11.

[69] Ibid., 11-12.

[70] Ibid., 15.

[71] Ibid., 16.

[72] Ibid., 17-18.

[73] Ibid.

[74] Ibid., 20, 22-23.

[75] Ibid., 20-21.

[76] Ibid., 21-24.

[77] Snyer, Bill and Bonna de la Cruz. "Gore Wants Additional $1 Billion for Veterans Critics Say Proposed Increases in Health Care Funding Fall Short, *The Tennessean* (Nashville) 27 July 1999, 1A.

[78] President Clinton, William Jefferson, Proclamation, " On Signing the Veteran's Millennium Health Care and Benefits Act," *Federal Register* 64 (30 November 1999): 2473, microfiche.

[79] "Feds Work to Protect Vets' Healthcare, *Dayton Daily News* (Dayton) 25 March 2000, 3A.

[80] Ibid.

CHAPTER 3

THE ROLE OF CONGRESSIONAL COMMITTEES

This chapter discusses the activities of certain congressional committees, such as House and Senate Veteran's Affairs Committees, in the formulation and passage of the Veteran's Millennium Health Care Act (VMHCA) of 1999. It also examines the floor proceedings of both chambers. The role of legislatiors, congressional committees and the full chambers are also analyzed.

The Bill in the House

During the first session of the 106th Congress, the House Committee on Veteran's Affairs was composed of seventeen (17) Republicans and fourteen (14) Democrats. Representative Bob Stump (R-AZ) was the chair of the Veteran's Affairs Committee. The Subcommittee on Hospitals and Health was chaired by Representative Cliff Stearns (R-FL). The subcommittee was composed of eight (8) GOP members and seven (7) Democratic members.[1]

The Veteran's Affairs Committee had jurisdiction over all of the GOP and Democratic measures that were incoporated into the veteran's health care and benefits reform legislation. It had jurisdiction over the provisions that covered long-term health care, respite care, adult day health care, educational benefits like the "GI Bill," pensions, and eligibility requirements for veterans, their spouses and dependents. The committee referred the veteran's bill to its Subcommittee on Hospitals and Health.

The Bill in the House Veteran's Affairs Subcommittee on Hospitals and Health

The subcommittee held two (2) hearings on the Veteran's Millennium Health Care Act (VMHCA). The first hearing was held on May 19, 1999 prior to the introduction of the bill. It is important to note that the language in the draft legislation was a result of a series of five committee hearings which the House Committee on Veteran's Affairs, in a joint session held with the Senate Committee on Veteran's Affairs. During these proceedings, various veteran's organizations presented their legislative proposals and objectives to the full committees. Many of these presentations highlighted and laid the groundwork for Congress' decision to revisit veteran's entitlement programs, particularly the veteran's health care system.

Prior to the introduction of VMHCA on the House floor, the subcomittee held a preliminary hearing to discuss House bill -- H.R. 2116 (draft legislation) on May 19, 1999. The hearing began with both the chairman and the ranking member emphasizing the importance of bi-partisan cooperation in considering this bill. During the debate in subcommittee, one issue that Democrats vigilantly contested was the provision that granted the Department of Veteran's Affairs the authority to increase copayments charged to veterans for health care services. Nonetheless, the Republican leadership was committed to allowing the department the discretion to increase copayment fees charged to veterans for medical care. Despite the opposition, Stearns indicated that the language was necessary in order to assist the Veteran's Administration in raising revenue so it might become less dependent on federal appropriations to administer the massive program. In fact, he argued that the increase in copayments would reduce the Department of Veteran's Affairs' dependence on federal funding. In short, he maintained, increases in copayments would increase the financial revenue available to the department to implement veteran's health care programs.[2]

The Veteran's Millennium Health Care Act emerged from the preliminary subcommittee hearing with four distinct objectives: (1) to reduce gaps in the veteran's eligibility law; (2) to ensure veterans receive the long-term health care they need; (3) to increase veteran's access to VA facilities and services; and (4) to reform the Veteran's Administration's health care system.[3]

On June 9, 1999, after having held a preliminary hearing on H.R. 2116 - the Veteran's Millennium Health Care Act (VMHCA) - Representative Ciff Stearns (R-FL) introduced the bill in the House. Later that day, the Veteran's Affairs Subcommitte on Hospitals and Health, with Stearns presiding as chairman, conducted a mark-up of the the bill. The subcommittee had jurisdiction over veteran's health care and benefit programs, i.e., pensions, life insurance, compensation, vocational rehabilitation, educational program, hospitals, medical care, treatment for veterans, the Soldier and Sailor Relief programs, readjustment programs for servicemen returning to civilian life, the veteran's housing program, and national cemeteries.[4]The legislation was proposed to overhaul major elements of the veteran's health care system. During the markup, the Republican and Democratic members of the subcommittee worked together in a bi-partisan fashion to stregthen and expand veteran's benefits, particularly medical care benefits. Members of the subcommittee worked diligently to expand veteran's services, while simultaneously allowing the VA discretion to determine how best to fulfill the federal mandates.

The markup session began with a call for bipartisan cooperation by both the chair, Representative Cliff Stearns (R-FL) and ranking member of the subcommittee Representative Lane Evans (D-IL).[5] During the subcommittee hearing, Democrats while supportive of the major elements and language of the bill, objected to language that would give the Department of Veteran's Affairs the discretion to increase the copayments for non-service related injuries and illnesses. At the hearings, veteran's organizations such as the Paralyzed Veterans Association and The Retired Enlisted Officers Association (TREA) expressed reservations about the manner in which the department would determine the new copayment schedule, as well as the amount of the increase. The Democrats on the subcommittee expressed concern that veterans would be unduly burdened by copayment increases for medical services administered by the Veteran's Administration. They submitted that many veteran's were even having difficulty paying their copayments as they were. The Republican leadership determined that the copayment language should remain in the bill; subcommittee chair Stearns (R-FL) disagreed and insisted on retianing the measure as a way to help the VA to reduce program costs. Congressional Republicans, further concluded the measure would further assist the department in becoming less dependent on budget allocations for program implementation.[6]

The mark-up session on H.R. 2116, however, turned out to be an exhibition of bipartisan cooperation. There was limited opposition from members of the Democratic Party because language from a bill previously introduced by ranking member Lane Evans (D-IL) was incorporated into the Veteran's Millennium Health Care Act. Representative Lane Evans (D-IL) introduced the legislation, but the GOP leadership had failed to act on the bill.[7] Finally, on June 9, 1999, the House Veteran's Affairs Subcommittee on Hospitals and Health approved the major provisions and passed it via a voice-vote. The legislation increased veteran's access and eligibility to medical facilities operated by the Department of Veteran's Affairs, and expanded eligibility of veterans for extended health care services and other veteran's benefits. Additionally, the bill: required the Veteran's Administration (VA) to maintain long-term care programs and to increase both home-care and community based care; provided special eligibility for medical care for veterans awarded the Purple Heart; authorized emergency care coverage for veterans; mandated that the Department of Veteran's Affairs make nursing care and nursing home care a mandatory part of its veteran's medical program; elevated the priority for VA medical care of military retirees; authorized the Department of Veteran's Affairs to sell or lease unused or obsolete medical facilities that threatened the quality of care and tended to waste departmental funds; established new outpatient facilities; provided for contracting out for hospital care when the department is unable to provide it for veterans; authorized the Department of Veteran's Affairs to set appropriate and affordable copayments for other non-service related care; empowered the department to create new sources of revenue to support the delivery of improved health care services.[8] The bill included provisions on veteran's health care and improving veteran's access to medical services administered by the U.S. Department of Veteran's Affairs. It was co-sponsored by 20 members to signal to their consituents and colleagues their commitment to veteran's health care issues and benefits. Co-sponsorship was crucial because it also signalled the level of support the legislation had in the chamber. Co-sponsorship of H.R. 2116 was bipartisan in nature; ten Republicans and ten Democrats cosponsored the reform bill. Following the introduction of this legislation, the bill was placed in the hopper. It was then referred to the House Committee on Veteran's Affairs by the Speaker of the House, Representative Denny Hastert's (R-IL) office.[9]

The Subcommittee on Hospitals and Health held its second hearing on the VMHCA. This one addressed the cost and impact of the veteran's reform package. The panel heard testimony from Paul Van de Water, Assistant Director of Budget Analysis for the Congressional Budget Office (CBO). He appeared before the subcommittee and presented cost estimates for the Veteran's Millennium Health Care Act. Other onlookers included Daniel Schoeps, a representative for the Veteran's Administration's Geriatric and Extended Care Strategic Healthcare Group, and Dr. Thomas Gaithwaite, the Department of Veteran's Affairs Undersecretary for Health.

Van de Water discussed the budgetary impact of the veteran's reform legislation. His presentation included discussion of both expected mandatory and discretionary spending for the bill.[10] The Department of Veteran's Affairs utilizes discretionary funds to administer its veteran's health care program. Funding for this program is provided annually in the Department of Veteran's Affairs and Housing Development (VA/HUD) appropriations bill. It is important to note that no matter what the veteran's program is authorized to spend, program expenditures are contingent upon federal dollars appropriated by Congress.

The cost estimate represented an analysis of the resources that would be necessary to carryout the veteran's entitlement program. Therefore, the Congressional Budget Office (CBO), estimate assumed that Congress would "fully" fund the program and that other programmatic activities would not be reduced to meet new federal mandates. As such Mr. Van de Water's testimony provided pertinent information about two aspects of the bill. He addressed the fiscal consequences associated with the veteran's reform bill. Second, his testimony discussed the impact the reform legislation would have on program enrollment.[11]

The Congressional Budget Office (CBO) suggested that the proposed legislation would cost the federal government approximately

$138 million in fiscal year 2000 and nearly $1.4 billion in fiscal year 2004. Van de Water testified that the provision to give priority status for medical care to veterans injured or disabled in combat would increase program spending more than $20 million each year. This projection was, of course, contingent upon Congress making additional appropriations available in the VA/HUD Appropraitions bill.[12]

The estimate assumed that the population of veterans disabled in combat was about the same as the number of veterans awarded a Purple Heart medal. According to the Department of Veteran's Affairs, there were roughly 500,000 recipients of the award who remain living. Therefore, Van de Water argued that half of them (250,000) would qualify for priority medical care due to a service-connected disability. He continued that many of these veterans would qualify for such care on the basis of their income because their earnings were not sufficient enough to bear the financial burden of long-term medial care. While 250,000 veterans were estimated as meeting the standards for the priority care, CBO reasoned that only a minute percentage (2%) would seek such services through the Veteran's Administration. Van de Water based his evaluation on the number of disabled veterans who received medical treatment on VA facilities in 1996. He did, however, recognize the likelihood that the percentage of veterans seeking medical treatment would increase under the veteran's reform legislation. [13] The law required the Veteran's Administration (VA) to treat disabled veterans before able bodied veterans. It stated that the Veteran's Administration was required to make medical services available, i.e., in-patient or hospital care, nursing home care and outpatient services. Mr. Van de Water noted that the VA provided nursing home care for close to 34,000 veterans each day. In addition, CBO projected that the Department of Veteran's Affairs, veteran's health administration, would be treating nearly 65,800 veterans daily who needed extended medical care services. These services, according to Van de Water, cost the department nearly $2.6 billion each year. Of the 65,800 veterans treated in VA facilities, roughly 11,000 of them suffered from service-connected disibilities which rendered them partially (50% or more) disabled. CBO analysis indicated that it would cost almost $1 billion a year. Therefore, extended medical care for disabled veterans would cost roughly $4 billion between fiscal year 2000 and 2004.[14]

The Congressional Budget Office, further, suggested the emergency care provision of H.R. 2116 would increase VA expenditures by $80 million in fiscal year 2000 alone. Mr. Van de Water contended that the Veteran's Administration (VA) would need to increase its spending by an additional $400 million in fiscal year 2004. This provision would be costly seeing as it mandated that the Department of Veteran's Affairs should reimburse veterans and medical treatment facilities for emergency treatment costs. The provision would force the VA to increase spending greatly because medical treatment provided in emergency rooms was dreadfully expensive. The Congressional Budget Office (CBO) based it determination on the rationale that veterans who sought medical treatment in emergency rooms were frequently admitted into the hospital. Moreover, the CBO suggested that almost two thirds of visits to emergency rooms made by veterans were ligitimate ones.[15]

The Veteran's Millennium Health Care Act (VMHCA) also required copayments from veterans for medical treatment not related to a service injury or disability. The copayments charged to veterans and collected by the VA would in turn be spent on providing additional long-term medical care for veterans. Based on Van de Water's testimony, the Department of Veteran's Affairs would collect around $0.3 billion in total payments by the year 2010.[16]

Another provision of the legislation extended eligibility to Vietnam veterans for "readjustment counseling from January 1, 2000 through January 1, 2003." Twenty percent of all patients enrolled in the program served in the Vietnam War. Their participation, according to CBO, costs the VA roughly $70 million in 1999. Van de Water estimated that this provision alone would increase program spending by virtually $34 million from year 2000 through 2004.[17]

The cost estimate for expanding outreach to homeless veterans suggested that it would cost the federal government an additional $520,000. The additional funds were needed to purchase vans to increase program outeach efforts. The VA could then, subsidize the purchase of vans to increase outreach efforts to homeless veterans. The Act also included a measure to extend the homeless veteran's program by making grants available to homeless shelters for veterans. The measure extended the availability of project grants from 1999 to 2002. The estimate prepared by the Congresssional Budget Office stated that this provision would increase VA spending by $6 million over a two year period (2000-2002). Van de Water said that the expansion of this program would cost an additional $37 million between fiscal years 2000 through 2004.[18]

The Veteran's Millennium Health Care Act (VMHCA) also proposed a pilot program that would provide medical treatment for eligible dependents of veterans. Under this mandate, the dependent or guardian of the dependent would be responsible for paying a fee for medical services. This was similar to other health insurance policies that provide coverage for an individual's dependent. Because the veteran's dependent was required to pay for services, Van de Water's presentation suggests that this particular measure would not dramatically increase program spending.[19]

The Act also mandated that the VA provide psychological counseling be made available to veterans who experienced sexual trauma or abuse. Under this measure, the program was extended for an additional year. According to the Congressional Budget Office (CBO) estimates that provision would require the VA to spend a few million dollars to implement the counseling program.[20]

The VMHCA also gave the Department of Veteran's Affairs the authority and discretion to spend any proceeds awarded to the federal government in lawsuits filed against the tobacco industry. Mr. Van de Water explained that if the government successfully won in litigation, the department might possibly, collect roughly $80 million. He maintained this type of "money-raising" would counterbalance departmental spending for the veteran's health care system and costly.[21]

Finally, in his testimony before the Subcommittee on Benefits, Paul Van de Water addressed the cost impact on intergovernmental agencies and the private sector. As previously mentioned, the legislation requires the VA to reimburse health care professionals for emergency treatment given to veterans enrolled in the veteran's health care program. While the provision was beneficial to veterans, it could potentially negatively impact private and intergovernmental agencies that gave medical treatment to veterans especially if a dispute were to arise over charges. In the event of a disagreement, Van de Water concluded that the veteran would not be financially liable for paying the hospital bill. Therefore, he testified that private sector and intergovernmental entities might suffer financial losses, if the VA's payment for emergency care services was lower than the amount billed for treatment.[22]

The Bill in the House Veteran's Affairs Subcommittee on Benefits

The House Veteran's Affairs Subcommittee on Benefits held two (2) hearings on a series of veteran's bills that were later incorporated into House bill - H.R. 2116. The subcommittee hearings allowed witnesses and members to discuss legislation that would add bronchiolo alveolar carcinoma to a list of cancers the government. The mandate required the Department of Veteran's Affairs to recognize and treat this form of cancer as service-connected illness or disease. The disease affected veterans who were exposed to radioactive materials during their military service. The Subcommittee also heard requests to increase the allowance given to veteran's dependent children and surviving spouses. Dependence and Indemnity Compensation was determined to be an appropriate benefit for surviving spouses of former Prisoners of War (POWs) who were disabled while serving the United States. Because these veterans (POWs) sustained injuries during their service, the subcommittee determined that it was only fitting that following their deaths financial assistance be made available to their families. This measure was drafted by Representative Stump (R-AZ), chairman of the full committee.[23]

The panel also considered legislation that would increase the quality of services available within VA operated medical treatment facilities. This proposal grew out of customer satisfaction survey that was conducted by the American Legion. The survey assessed: (1) assess the timeliness of service; (2) veteran's satisfaction with the manner in which the benefits programs were administered; (3) overall quality of medical care services; and (4) program coordination and organization in implementing program changes. The language drafted by Represenatative Lane Evans (D-IL), the ranking member of the Committee on Veteran's Affairs was incorporated. He did so out of concern that veterans appeared to lack confidence in the Veteran's Administration's ability to effectively implement needed programs.[24] The legislative measure considered, during the subcommittee hearing, was co-sponsored by Representatives Stump (R-AZ), Smith (R-NJ), and Bilirakis (R-FL).

On June 16, 1999, the Subcommittee on Benefits held a hearing on another series of legislative proposals on veteran's benefit issues. One provided an opportunity for witnesses and members of the panel to discuss veteran's issues like expanding the fund-raising authority of the American Battle Monuments Commission. The subcommittee deemed this necessary in order that the Commission could raise enough capital to erect the World War II (WWII) Memorial in the nation's capital, Washington, D.C.[25] Another authorized appropriations to increase program outreach to homeless veterans. Additionally, the Subcommittee on Benefits listened to testimony on making Riverside National Cemetary, located in California, a national memorial in recognition of recipients of the Medal of Honor.[26] What's more, the panel considered legislation to require that an assessment be conducted on cemetaries operated by the Veteran's Administration. Consequently, the subcommittee considered creating additional national cemetaries for veterans. This was due to the limited burial space available in national cemetaries. The legislative proposals covered during the hearing were sponsored by Stump, chairman of the full committee and Evans, ranking member of the committee.[27]

The Subcommittee on Benefits concluded its actions and favorably reported the series of bills to the full committee for its consideration. Both the Subcommitte chair, Jack Quinn (R-NY) and ranking member, Bob Filner (D-CA) expressed the sentiment that the bills would greatly improve the lives of millions of veterans and their familes. They also recommended that the full committee consider including the series of measures in the Veteran's Millennium Health Care Act (VMHCA).[28]

The Bill in the House Veteran's Affairs Committee

On July 15, 1999, the Committee on Veteran's Affairs began its mark-up session on the Veteran's Millennium Health Care bill. This bill, which represented the first attempt by Congress, in more than twenty years, to develop a comprehensive veteran's health care and benefits package transformed major sections of the nations veteran's health care system. Prior to the passage of this bill, Congress and the Veteran's Affairs Committee handled veteran's programs in a piecemeal fashion; legislation dealing with Veteran's Affairs were dealt with one at a time. For example, legislation dealing with veteran's copayments for medical treatment, long-term health care, emergency care services, home care services and the like were considered independently of one another. Thus, the Veteran's Millennium Health Care Act (VMHCA) represented one of the first attempts, in over twenty years, to address conditions plaguing America's veterans in a holistic fashion.[29]

Despite minor differences between the Republicans and Democrats on the committee, the members compromised and handled the bill with mutual aid. The Democratic membership of the committee agreed to the inclusion of the copayment provision which allowed the Department of Veteran's Affairs to increase veteran's copayments for non-service related illnesses. As previously mentioned, the Democratic members of the committee initially opposed increasing veteran's copayments because many veterans could not afford the copayments. On the other hand, the Republican leadership favored increased copayments; the committee viewed it as a means by which the Veteran's Administration could become less dependent on government appropriations. Chairman Stump (R-AZ) of the Committee on Veteran's Affairs ruled that the majority of the committee, by voice-vote, approved the bill on July 15, 1999.

The next day, the Committee reported the Veteran's Millennium Health Care Act (VMHCA) to the full House.[30] Representative Cliff Stearns (R-FL) reaffirmed the significance of the Act (VMHCA) on the House floor. He maintained that the bill offered a blueprint that would assist the Veteran's Administration (VA) to better implement veteran's programs, particularly the veteran's health care system. The legislator asserted that the bill recognized the Department of Veteran's Affairs' authority to close medical facilities it determined to be underused or obsolete. However, he noted that the Act included safeguards to ensure that the VA could not arbitrarily close medical facilities. Consequently, special language was integrated in the legislation as a means of deterring the Department of Veteran's Affairs from closing a health care facility and "walking away from its responsibilities."[31]

The Representative also argued that the bill would provide a blueprint for the future implementation of veteran's programs while simultaneously saving appropriation dollars. He maintained that the revenue saved could be re-invested in new and improved medical facilities and improved benefits. Furthermore, the Congressman noted that the Veteran's Millennium Health Care Act (VMHCA) would expand long-term care, increase veteran's access to services and benefits (i.e., coverage of emergency care and priority status granted to veterans who received a Purple Heart Award).[32]

Additionally, Stearns (R-FL) pointed to the timelines and necessity of the bill. He highlighted a study conducted by the Government Accounting Office (GAO), which estimated that the Department of Veteran's Affairs would waste roughly $20 billion over the next five years on inefficient or obsolute programs. The report, therefore, recommended a few capital management strategies that would forstall that possibility. The report by GAO also claimed that the Veteran's Health Administration had been unsuccessful in implementing a realignment process which could have made it more efficient. It therefore suggested the Administration (1) consolidate its services when possible, (2) develop partnership with health care providers, and (3) replace obsolete medical facilities with renovated or newly constructed ones. At the conclusion of the proceeding, Representative Stearns (R-FL) stated that the information presented by witnesses would be used to modify the VMHCA. He urged his colleagues to favorably report the bill.[33]

In an effort to prompt support for H.R. 2116, Representative Bob Filner (D-CA) asserted that the Act improved the VA health care system by extending long-term care and emergency care services. Furthermore, he noted that the bill provided sexual trauma counseling for veterans who had been sexually harassed. He argued that the Veteran's Millennium Health Care Act increased veteran's access to health services and other benefits such as the "GI Bill" which provided educational assistance to veterans. Additionally, the Congressman articulated support for a provision in the bill that would ensure chiropractic services to veterans. The provision also ensured that the Veteran's Administration (VA) would work with licensed chiropractic physicians in an attempt to improve access to chiropractic services. This provision was significant because it changed the departmental policy which failed to provide such services.[34]

Representative Filner (D-CA) affirmed the language to establish a biomedical research facility for the Veteran's Administration's San Diego Healthcare System. Researchers at the facility would conduct research projects on hypertension, Auto Immune Deficiency Syndrome (AIDS), Parkinson's Disease and diabetes. He specified support for VMHCA because it addressed key issues facing the health care needs of veterans as well as the needs of the Department of Veteran's Affairs.[35] It is worth noting that Filner had a personal stake in the legislation; his strong support of the bill was not offered for totally altruistic reasons. Opposing the legislation would have cost him, and his constituents the medical research facility which would accommodate much needed medical research as well as create new jobs for his constituents.[36]

The House Debates the Bill

The full chamber formally began consideration and debate on the Veteran's Millennium Health Care Act on September 21, 1999. It is important to note that members of the House of Represenatives spoke on the floor about the significance of the proposed veteran's legislation prior to it being favorably reported by the Committee on Veteran's Affairs. As the aforementioned suggests, members of the Veteran's Affairs Committee and Subcommittee on Hospitals and Health discussed the bill's provisions and their merits. This was done in an effort to increase awareness of legislative goals of the committee and gain feedback from non-committee members. Such feedback and dialogue helps committee members address concerns that might become troublesome when considered by the full chamber. The members spent enormous time addressing issues related to the need for increased medical services and benefits for America's veterans. This is illustrated by the fact that Republicans and Democrats, alike, communicated support for the veteran's bill.

Additionally, Representative Bob Stump (R-AZ), chairman of the Veteran's Affairs' Committee, made a motion to suspend the rules and pass the bill in its amended form. The motion to suspend the rules limited the amount of time permitted for debate on the bill. Under suspension of the rules, the Act was debated for forty-five minutes. The debate and consideration of H.R. 2116 did not allow members of the House to offer amendments to the legislation. It is important to note that typically only non-controversial bills are considered under the suspension of rules. Unfortunately, the floor debate is not available to the public nor was it printed in the *Congressional Record*. However, the arguments made by various members of the House and Senate are discussed later in this chapter.

Upon the conclusion of the debate, a voice-vote was ordered - yeas and nays were ordered, however, the vote was temporarily postponed. The Republican and Democratic leadership met and resolved the conflict surrounding the bill. During the late afternoon on

September 21, 1999, it was brought back to the floor and another motion was made to suspend the rules and pass the bill. In order for the bill to pass under a suspension of the rules, two-thirds of the Representatives in the House needed to vote in favor of the legislation. The Veteran's Millennium Health Care Act passed the House by a vote of 369 to 46. It is worth noting that eighteen members of the House were absent and failed to register their votes in favor of or in opposition to the bill. Among those absent were seven (7) Republicans and eleven (11) Democrats.[37] The House version of the Act was sent to the United States Senate for consideration.

Representative Eva Clayton (D-NC), one of the Democrats who missed the vote on the bill, provided an explanation for her absence. The Congresswoman maintained that she missed the vote on the comprehensive veteran's bill because she was working in her congressional district assisting victims of "Hurricane Floyd"; the hurricane left many of her constituents homeless and devastated. Although she missed the vote, Clayton stressed that she would have voted in favor of the bill had she been present.[38]

Additionally, Representative Steny Hoyer (D-MD) noted that he had inadvertently voted against H.R. 2116. He noted his intent to vote for the bill because it was the first time Congress tried to address the issue of long-term care benefits for veterans. Furthermore, he maintained that the provision of the bill which provided long-term care benefits for veterans classified as having a "50 percent disability or greater" was a much needed policy change.[39] The Congressman also liked the provision covering the costs of emergency care for uninsured veterans. According to him, that was significant because it changed the preexisting policy that denied emergency care services to veterans. The member declared that the passage of the Veteran's Millennium Health Care Act - H.R. 2116 was a significant effort towards addressing the diverse health care needs of veterans.[40]

On September 24, 1999, Congressman Harold Rogers (R-KY) expressed his support. He pointed out that he supported the Act in view of the fact that many of the provisions were long overdue. For example, Rogers asserted that the reform measures included in the legislation ensured the continuation of health care services made available to veterans well into the next century. However, he was staunchly opposed to Section 203 -- the Veteran's Trust Fund, which required that a percentage of revenue recovered from tobacco manufacturers from lawsuits filed by the United States government, be transferred to an account within the Department of Treasury. Funds received from government lawsuits against the tobacco lobby would be placed in a special account that would later be used to provide treatment to veterans suffering from illnesses related to tobacco products and smoking. He argued that the language in the bill further legitimizes federal lawsuits against tobacco companies.

Cosequently, Rogers' opposition to section 203 in the House version of the Veteran's Millennium Health Care Act stemmed from his belief that lawsuits were politically motivated. He also added that such litigation would be legally suspect and would unfairly target manufacturers and merchants who sold tobacco products. Thus, Representative Rogers cautioned that if section 203 of the bill were included in the conference report, the provision would cause irreparable harm to the farm economies of many states, particularly tobacco farmers in his district. He, furthermore, argued that the section was unnecessary because it failed to assist in improving the delivery of medical and health care services to veterans. Despite his opposition to this particular provision in the bill, he acknowledged that the other major provisions of the bill were well written and sound. Finally, he submitted that it was for these reasons that he supported the legislation.[41]

Following the passage of the Act (VMHCA) on September 22, 1999, Representative Ron Packard (R-CA) indicated why he voted for the bill. He considered the provisions in the bill that called for expanded veteran eligibility for medical services and improved home-care services extremely important. He also noted his support for provisions in the bill that required the Department of Veteran's Affairs to develop and implement a national long-term care program. The Congressman stated that although the Veteran's Administration/Housing and Urban Development Appropriations (VA/HUD) bill totaling $196 billion was passed, representing an increase of $1.7 billion earmarked especially for veteran's health care services, he still felt the Veteran's Administration was nevertheless underfunded. In fact, Representative Packard argued that if the Veteran's Millennium Health Care bill was properly funded in the appropriations process, the nation would have indicated its appreciation to Congress for its commitment to provide veterans with the health care services they desperately needed. He maintained that while the legislation was a step towards addressing problems concerning the implementation of veteran's health care, Congress' commitment to veteran's health care would be apparent when funding for the Department of Veteran's Affairs is increased significantly.[42]

The Bill in the Senate

House bill H.R. 2116 was received by the Senate on September 22, 1999. The bill was referred to the Committee on Veteran's Affairs. The committee was composed of seven (7) Republicans and five (5) Democrats.[43] The bill aimed to improve the overal implementation of veteran's benefits. The legislation emphasized increased veteran's access to long-term health and nursing home care services, respite care and priority medical treatment for Purple Heart recipients.[44]

The Senate Veteran's Affairs Committee deliberated over the comprehensive legislative package of veteran's entitlements. Members of the Republican majority and the Democratic party joined in an effort to expand these programs. It was a show of solidarity for America's veterans. Therefore, the committee worked with a sense of bipartisan cooperation. The Veteran's Millennium Health Care Act was discharged by the committee after a brief meeting. The bill was released from committee by unanimous consent.

The Act was considered on the Senate floor by unanimous consent, November 5, 1999. Shortly thereafter, Senators Domenici (R-NM) proposed a substitute amendment to House bill H.R. 2116. He did so on behalf of Senator Arlen Specter (R-PA), sponsor of Senate Amendment 2541. Following debate on the merits of the amendment, the Senate agreed to Specter's substitute amendment by Unianimous Consent. Senator Specter's amendment included measures which established the following:

1. a pilot program to assist the Department of Veteran's Affairs determine the most cost-effective method of delivering long-term care to veterans;
2. priority status for veterans who received the Purple Heart award;
3. a new policy to allow flat grave markers in national cemetaries and extended the operation of the Santa Fe National Cemetary in New Mexico;

4. required the Department of Veteran's Affairs to operate specialized programs in the area of "Post-Traumatic Stress Disorder" in an attempt to enhance the implementation of veteran's mental health services;
5. modified the manner in which construction grants would be awarded; and
6. established reimbursement for emergency care services for veterans granted priority status.[45]

The creation of pilot programs was based on the amendment inserted in the Veteran's Long-Term Care Enhancement Act by Senator John Rockefeller (D-WV). The measure mandated the department to develop programs that would help determine the most cost-effective methods of providing health care including assisted living services to veterans. The Department of Veteran's Affairs was therefore instructed to begin gathering data and also develop pilot programs within the department or through cooperative arrangements with community health care providers who normally did not treat veterans. While Congress recognized that the Department had developed significant expertise in long-term care, it was equally cognizant of the fact that the department had failed to push its program development beyond the current medical and health care needs of veterans.[46]

Senator Rockefeller's amendment also established a specific eligibility for veterans who received a Purple Heart award. It is important to note that this provision was taken from legislation previously introduced by Senator Charles "Chuck" Robb (D-VA). According to the Military Order of the Purple Heart there were, at the time, approximately 500,000 veterans who had received the award. Approximately 250,000 of those so honored qualified for priority care based on their service-connected disability or income level.[47]

The amendment also included a provision that extended the viability of the Santa Fe National Cemetery located in Senator Pete Domenici's state of New Mexico. This provision permited flat grave markers to be used to identify burial sites. Flat markers are engraved with information about the deceased; they markers are utilized in national cemeteries, specifically the Santa Fe National Cemetery. This provision changed the department's policy that stipulated that only upright or standing grave markers be used in national cemeteries. The reasoning behind this change lies in the fact that flat grave markers would extend the viability of national cemeteries and require less space. Therefore, by switching to flat markers the amendment ensured that the national cemetery would remain viable or operational through 2008. This policy was endorsed by the New Mexico Chapter of the American Legion, the Veterans of Foreign Wars and the Albuquerque Chapter of the Retired Enlisted Officers' Association.[48]

The Senate version of the bill also mandated that the Department of Veteran's Affairs must improve its delivery of specialized mental health services to veterans. It targeted services for veteran's suffering from "Post-Traumatic Stress Disorder (PTSD)" and substance abuse disorders. Additionally, the bill called on Congress to appropriate $15 million in funding to finance Veterans Integrated Service Networks (VISNs) and individual veterans medical facilities that provided specialize mental health services. Furthermore, the language also ensured that grant funding, separate from VISN funding, should be increased by $15 million above the department's current spending level on mental health programs.[49]

Finally, the Senate amendment to H.R. 2116 modified the manner in which the Veteran's Administration's (VA) construction grants were awarded in 2000. The language in the Senate substitute amendment reshaped the provision and placed emphasis on grant proposals to renovate or maintain existing veteran's medical facilities, whereas, the House version of the bill authorized the Department of Veteran's Affairs to sell, lease, close old or obsolete veteran's medical facilities. In other words, the House version supported the department's policy which called for the reorganization and closure of veteran's medical facilities during the 1980s.

As a result, Senate Amendment 2541 mandated that precedence in awarding construction grants be given to grant proposals geared towards the maintenance of facilities operated and owned by the Veteran's Administration. It restored the eligibility of State operated veteran's homes which typically sought grants to fund renovation or maintenance projects. However, the House version would have made state operated veteran's homes ineligible to receive funding because it placed greater emphasis on grant proposals requesting funds to build new veteran's facilities. Consequently, the Senate amendment attempted to preserve the original intent of the House bill while ensuring that grant recipients would not lose funding due to a change in the manner in which construction grants would have been evaluated. Hence, directors of state operated veteran's homes are required to comply with the new criteria for construction grants for fiscal year 2001.[50]

Finally, the amendment incorporated a provision from the Veterans Acess to Emergency Care Act of 1999 previously introduced by Senator Tom Daschle (D-SD), the minority leader for the Democractic party. The emergency care access provision authorized the Veteran's Administration (VA) to offer emergency care reimbursement payents on behalf of veterans granted priority status. However, veterans must have received VA health services for at least two years prior to the emergency hospital visit. Moreover, veterans are eligible for reimbursement for emergency care payments when they lack medical insurance. Thus, the provision is signifiigant because it ensured that veterans who lacked medical coverage would receive medical care in cases of emergency. As a result, the legislation encouraged veterans to seek emergency care services when necessary, rather than go without treatment because they lacked of medical coverage.[51] Generally, failure to seek medical treatment resulted in further exacerbation of an illness.

As a result of the fact that the two bodies passed different versions of the veteran's bill. The Senate sent a message to the House requesting a conference. A Conference Committee was formed and Senators Arlen Specter (R-PA), Jay Rockefeller (D-WV), and Strom Thurmond (R-SC) were appointed as Senate conferees. Similarly, the Speaker of the House of Representatives, appointed Representatives Bob Stump (R-AZ), Christopher Smith (R- NJ), Jack Quinn (R-NY), Cliff Stearns (R-FL), Lane Evans (D-IL), Corrine Brown (D-FL), and Michael Doyle (D-PA.) to the conference committee on the Veteran's Millennium Health Care Act.[52] It is worth noting that five (5) of the aforementioned conferees - Specter, Thurmond, Stump, Stearns, and Evans are veterans of the military. Accordingly, they exhibited an enormous commitment to veteran's issues. In addition to these members, there are a number of veterans serving in the 106th Congress. A significant number of members in both chambers served in the military and were officers with ranks from private to captain. In all, of the 345 veterans holding seats in the House 119 were veterans. Furthermore, there were 35 members of the Senate that served in the U.S. military.[53]

The Bill in Conference Committee

The House and Senate members of the committee met to negotiate the final version of the bill. Procedurally, there are two ways in which the conference process of reaching a final agreement on a bill occurs. The chambers may exchange amendments or conferees are appointed to resolve the differences and draft a final version.[54] In the case of the Veteran's Millennium Health Care Act (VMHCA), both the House and Senate appointed conferees to resolve exiting differences in the House and Senate versions of the bill.

Few rules are imposed on the conference committee because the committee acts as a negotiating forum. Thus, conferees have discretion to decide how they will conduct such proceedings. Both chambers allow conferees considerable latitude and discretion regarding the content of the agreements reached in a conference committee. Nevertheless, House conferees are expected to limit their discussions to the issues with which disagreement exists. Alternatively, the Senate imposes even fewer restrictions on the policy agreements that conferees reach.[55]

The Conference Committee convened for three days, November 8 through November 10, 1999, to resolve differences in the House and Senate versions of the legislation. Members of the committee agreed to file the conference report on November 10, 1999. The House and Senate Veteran's Affairs' Committees have yet to make available a report on the closed conference committee proceeding. Therefore, it is impossible at this time to surmise precisely what took place in the committee deliberations. However, close examination of the conference bill and the Senate's substitute amendment allows one to deduce that House conferees agreed to accept the language in Senate Amendment 2541, sponsored by Senator Specter (R-PA). Once the conference committee agreed to the language of Conference Report 106-476, it was dissolved and the report was forwarded to the full chambers for their approval.

The House Considers the Conference Bill

The House of Representatives began its consideration of the conference bill on November 16, 1999. When a conference committee approves its report, the next stage in the legislative process is for it to be presented to the full House and the full Senate for consideration. conference reports can only be filed in one chamber at a time. conference reports are granted a high privilege under House Rule XXVIII clause 1 (a) which allows the papers to be presented or filed at almost any time while the House is in session. However, there are three exceptions to this procedure which include: (1) when the *Journal* is being read; (2) the roll is being called; and (3) the House is divided on a question. These exemptions apply only when the House is resolved into the Committee of the Whole.[56] These exceptions did not affect House consideration of conference report 106-476.

The legislation was brought to the House floor for consideration. Normally, conference reports are considered under the "one-hour rule." House Rule XXVIII, clause 2 (a) requires that the hour be equally divided between the Democratic and Republican Parties. Moreover, the rule requires the debate to be controlled by the majority and minority parties. If the bill managers from both parties (chairman of the committee and ranking committee member), support the conference report, the rule provides that a member who opposes the final version has the right to control one-third of the hour, if he or she chooses. Although recognition of members who oppose legislation is not dependent upon party affiliation, priority is given to a member of the "Conference Committee" who opposes the bill. The amount of time allowed for debate may be extended through a unanimous consent, a special rule or by defeating the previous question on the conference report. Thus, the House of Representatives may choose to accept or reject the conference report.[57]

If the report is rejected by the second chamber, the rules governing the handling of conference reports require that the legislation be re-negotiated. Thus, one chamber must propose a new position to the other chamber as an amendment. In addition, the chamber could request a new conference committee. Moreover, in the event that the conference report is either recommitted to committee or rejected and sent to a new conference committee, all of the issues originally sent to conference must be reconsidered by conferees.[58]

It is worth noting that the House bypassed the standard rules of debate governing legislation by considering House bill H.R. 2116 under "suspension of the rules, as moved by Representative Bob Stump (R-AZ), chairman of the House Committee on Veteran's Affairs. The motion was agreed to by a voice vote and the veteran's reform bill passed as amended by the conference committee.[59]

Subsequently, members of the House of Represenatatives provided floor statement for the record explaining the manner in which they voted on the Veteran's Millennium Health Care Act (VMHCA). Their statements provide insight into the rationale for their support of the bill. For example, Representative Sheila Jackson-Lee (D-TX) supported H.R. 2116, the Veteran's Millennium Health Care Act because the bill would have a positive effect on the approximately 1,700,000 veterans who reside in Texas and also improve the quality of life for veterans throughout the country. It is important to add that the Houston Department of Veteran's Affairs Medical Center is located in her congressional district. Furthermore, the Center served over 50,000 veterans in her district at the time the Act passed.[60]

Additionally, she maintained that VMHCA offered comprehensive reforms to improve the Veteran's Administration's (VA) health care system. The reforms included in the Veteran's Millennium Health Care Act required the VA to increase extended care through use of improved home-care and community-based options for veterans. The legislation also mandated that the VA provide nursing home care to veterans through 2003. The member stated that the Act removed the six-month time limit which previously existed on VA day care services.[61] Therefore, veterans in need of day care services could receive such treatment as long as they needed them without being forced to leave the facility.

Representative Sheila Jackson-Lee (D-TX) stated that while the United States honors veterans on November 11 of each calendar year, the country should recognize the sacrifice and contribution made by veterans each day. She added that American veterans had led the nation against those who threatened the values and interests of the United States. Finally, the Congresswoman asserted that the Veteran's Millennium Health Care Act sent a message to America's veterans that when they "serve our nation we will answer the plea of President Lincoln 'to care for him who shall have borne the battle'."[62]

Although Representative Michael Doyle (D-Penn.) voted in favor of the conference bill, he expressed his disappointment regarding the fact that the several provisions of the House version of H.R. 2116 that he liked were not included in the final bill. For example, the conference report failed to include provisions which gave employees and veteran's organizations the authority to participate in the Veteran's Administration's decision-making process and planning practices. He also noted that the language for employee protection, hospital guidelines, cost-benefit analysis and oversight provisions were not included in the conference bill. Doyle asserted that the inclusion of such provisions would have significantly improved the Act's intentions and would have made the legislation less susceptible to inconsistent application or interpretation. Nonetheless, Representative Doyle maintained that while the conference bill was less than perfect, the Veteran's Millennium Health Care Act was worthy of support.[63]

Representative Christopher Smith (R-NJ), a member of the conference committee, also supported the conference report. During consideration of the bill in the House of Representatives, he expressed his appreciation for the fact that his proposal to add "bronchiolo alveolar carcinoma" to the Department of Veteran's Affairs list of radiogenic cancers was included in the conference bill. Consequently, the Department of Veteran's Affairs would recognize the newly added form of cancer as a service connected disease. Representative Smith (R-NJ) had attempted to have the form of cancer added to the department's list for ten years. During the 104th and 105th Congresses, the House passed legislation introduced by the Congressman that would have added "bronchiolo alveolar carcinoma" to the list of recognized cancers for which veterans could receive treatment; his efforts were successful when he negotiated the inclusion of "bronchiolo alveolar carcinoma" in the new law. The measure was deemed necessary because VA denied claims filed by veterans who requested treatment for bronchiolo alveolar carcinoma. Consequently, the new law caused a shift in policy by requiring the Department of Veteran's Affairs to provide medical treatment for veterans who were in contact with atomic materials during their military duty aor duties.[64]

Congressman Smith (R-NJ) explained his interest in the type of cancer developed out of an attempt his office made to assist a constituent by the name of Tom McCarthy. His wife requested assistance on behalf of her husband who was a veteran in the Navy having served as a navigator in Operation Wigwam. The naval exercise was one in which an underwater atomic test was conducted in the Pacific Ocean. He had been exposed to atomic materials when the test produced a mist which he inhaled. After years of respiratory problems, Tom McCarthy was diagnosed with bronchiolo alveolar carcinoma.

At the time of Smith's inquiries, the Veteran's Administration did not recognized the cancer as a service connected injury. Consequently, Tom McCarthy's family was required to bear the financial burden of paying for his cancer treatments. Despite their pleading, the Veteran's Administration denied their claim. The Department of Veteran's Affairs maintained that it was not obligated to do so since the cancer Mr. McCarthy contracted was not covered under the health care program. During the time Smith was working to get the cancer added to the department's list of cancers, Tom McCarthy died from the disease. He lived nearly twenty-five years after initially being exposed to atomic materials during Operation Wigwam. At the time of his death, he was in his early forties. As a result of this case, the language included in the new law made veterans suffering from bronchiolo alveolar carcinoma eligible for VA cancer treatment.[65] In addition, the Department of Veteran's Affairs can no longer deny that veterans were exposed to atomic materials in Operation Wigwam. The VA must now provide medical treatment for veterans suffering from that disease.

Additionally, Representative Christopher Smith of New Jersey, authored a respite care provision, which was incorporated into the conference bill. For the first time in the history of veteran's entitlement programs, Congress gave the Department of Veteran's Affairs the ability to "contract out" respite care services. Prior to the passage of H.R. 2116, when a veteran care giver, i.e. spouse or adult child, needed a break from providing home-care for the veteran, etc., the only alternative the caregiver had was to wait for a bed to become available in a VA facility or state operated nursing home. This alternative placed an extra burden on families to transport the veteran to a facility. Consequently, during fiscal year 1998, the Department of Veteran's Affairs received only 232 cases requesting nursing home services.[66]

According to the Caregiver Assistance Network, family caregivers provide approximately 85 percent of all home-care or nursing care in the United States. A California statewide survey performed by the Family Caregiver Alliance indicated that 58 percent of family caregivers showed signs of clinical depression. On average, family members spent approximately 11 hours per day caring for elderly family members. Thus, the new law gave the department the ability to contract out such services and thereby increasing the quality of life for veterans, their families and caregivers.[67]

The Conference Bill in the Senate

The conference report and the manager's bill statement were submitted to the Senate on November 17, 1999. This other body delayed action so the House could complete its action on the conference bill. As previously mentioned, the Rules dictate that only one chamber can consider a conference report at a time. Hence, the Senate began its consideration of the conference bill on November 19, 1999, following passage in the House.

Senator Arlen Specter (R-Penn.) urged the Senate to pass the conference bill. In an effort to substantiate the significance of the Veteran's Millennium Health Care Act (VMHCA), the Senator noted the bill's 74 substantive provisions aimed at improving the veteran's health care system. He argued that the legislation required the Veteran's Administration (VA) to provide improved long-term care services to veterans. The previous law, he continued, allowed the VA to provide long-term care in a discretionary manner - supplied on the basis of available space in facilities. He acknowledged the fact that the Department of Veteran's Affairs had provided nursing care to approximately 13,000 veterans per day at an annual cost of $1.1 billion, and provided private nursing home care for 6,000 veterans a day at an annual cost of $316.8 million. He also stated that the Veteran's Administration (VA) subsidized nursing-care or home-care services for 14,000 veterans per day in state operated nursing home facilities in addition to the Administration (VA) providing non-institutional alternatives to nursing home care at an annual cost of $154 million. Despite all of these, the Department could do better. The new law, he observed, would make that possible.[68]

Senator Specter (R-PA) expressed his satisfaction with the long-term care provisions in VMHCA. He also observed that veterans typically attempted to avoid or delay nursing home care services because of the enormous cost. Specter maintained that H.R. 2116 assured that non-institutional alternatives such as home-based services would be made available to veterans and their families. The bill entitled all veterans who enrolled in the veterans health program eligibility for primary care services, adult day care, home-based services and home health visits to receive them. These alternatives provided veterans with services that improve their quality of life while simultaneously allowing the administration to cut the costs of implementing programs.[69]

Senator Specter (R-PA) noted that the bill provided coverage for emergency care for all veterans who did not have medical or health care coverage. The Senator argued that the "emergency care" provision was critical to the health of veterans who lacked medical insurance. He stated that the significance of the provision laid in the fact that the legislation would ensure that veterans who relied solely on the VA to supply their health care needs would be eligible to receive emergency care services. The Veteran's Administration policy prior to the passage of the Veteran's Millennium Health Care Act (VMHCA) failed to provide such services for veterans. Therefore, veterans in need of emergency treatment would either: (1) go to a VA facility the following day; (2) pay for emergency care themselves; or (3) not seek treatment for their condition. Due to this, veterans would typically postponed medical treatment because they could not afford to pay for emergency care services. The Senator pointed out that such situations had caused many veterans to suffer through their illness until they could receive treatment at a VA operated community health care facility at a later date. The lack of access to emergency care, he continued, had further exascerbated their illness and injuries of veterans because they were not entitled to emrgency care services.[70]

In addition, Senator Specter was pleased that the legislation included positively enhanced services for older veterans. He was equally elated that Congress also responded to the needs of young veterans. He recalled that earlier in the 106th Congress, the Senate passed legislation to significantly improve veterans benefits under the "Montgomery GI Bill," but budgetary constraints led conferees to postpone any major effort to overhaul the "GI Bill" until the second session of the 106th Congress.[71]

Another Senator, Pete Domenici (R-NM) addressed his colleagues to share his reasons for supporting the legislation. His foremost reason for supporting the Veteran's Millennium Health Care Act (VMHCA) was that it required the VA to improve its delivery of services to veterans. He expressed a particular interest in the language aimed at extending the operation of the Santa Fe National Cemetery in New Mexico even though it was projected that the cemetery would run out of burial space for veterans at the end of fiscal year 2000. The Senator reasoned that at the very least veterans deserved to be buried at a National Cemetery. The closure, he continued, would have been extremely problematic for many families whose loved ones were burried in national cemeteries. It would have posed an even greater problem for families who wished to bury their loved one in a national cemetery. He was pleased that the provision in H.R. 2116 would compel the Department of Veteran's Affairs to change its policy of permitting only upright headstones at grace sites and allow the use of flat grave markers. This would extend the cemetery's lifespan into the fiscal year 2008.[72]

Senator John Rockefeller (D-WV) urged his colleagues to support the conference bill, arguing that the bill covered a broad spectrum of veterans issues (i.e., long-term care, improved educational benefits, and emergency care coverage). Additionally, he noted that approximately 35 percent of the veteran's population was 65 years of age or older. Consequently, the Veteran's Millennium Health Care Act directed the Veteran's Administration (VA) to provide extended care, nursing care to veterans in need of such care due to service-connected illnesses and injuries.[73]

House bill H.R. 2116 also included a provision introduced by Senator Rockefeller in the Veteran's Long-Term Care Enhancement Act of 1999. The provision mandated that the Secretary of the Department of Veteran's Affairs to implement a series of pilot programs within the next three years. The programs were designed to determine the most effective means for the department to meet the long-term care needs of veterans. The mandate required the department to offer veterans improved care through either cooperative arrangements with community health care providers or within the VA health care system. Senator Rockefeller noted that the purpose of the pilot program was to assist the Department of Veteran's Affairs evaluate various approaches of meeting the long-term care needs of veterans, as well as facilitating the development of additional approaches to long-term health care. Finally, Senator Rockefeller (D-WV) expressed a particular interest in Section 117 of the Veteran's Millennium Health Care Act which addressed mental health care services provided by the Department.[74]

Equally significant was Senator Olympia Snowe's (R-MN) support for the Veteran's Millennium Health Care Act Conference Report. Although, she expressed her support for the bill, she also noted her reservations regarding the manner in which VA construction grants were awarded. She expressed concern over language she believed threatened to jeopardize millions of federal grant dollars for her consituents in Veteran's Homes administered by the state of Maine. However, the conferees were able to negotiate a balance between the House and Senate versions of the bill and reached an acceptable compromise. Senator Snowe (R-MN) argued that the modified provision restructured the manner in which VA construction grants would be awarded. Unlike the House version, the restructured provision placed emphasis on renovating existing health care facilities. The House version of the bill authorized the Department of Veteran's Affairs to sell or lease to the public old and obsolete veteran's facilities. Hence, the revised provision mandated that the Veteran's Administration's (VA) maintenance projects take precedence over proposals to build new facilities. She argued that the language in the House version of the bill made a number of state operated veteran's homes ineligible for funding, despite the fact that their directors had already filed applications under the previous law. The Senator noted that, during the then ongoing grant process, the interests of states, with pending grant application, that were awaiting the announcement of awards. Their interest were protected because all pending applications were assessed based on the previous criteria and not criteria spelled out in H.R. 2116. However, grant applications submitted by states seeking funding for fiscal year 2001 would be required to submit their applications based on those stipulated in the 1999 law. Thus, grant applications were evaluated based on the criteria that existing prior to the decision to modify the criteria states must fulfill to obtain funding. This adjustment was made and ensured that the intent of the House version of the Veteran's Millennium Health Care Act was retained. The House version of the bill gave the Department of Veteran's Affairs greater discretion to close obsolete or underused VA medical facilitates and build new medical facilities. The conference bill ensured that state veteran homes would not lose grant funds for the fiscal year 2000. However, state operated veteran's homes would be responsible for adhering to the new grant application criteria when attempting to acquire funds in fiscal year 2001.[75]

The Senator noted another reason why she voted for the VMHCA was the provision on sexual abuse. The Department of Defense data, she said, indicated that at least 55 percent of active duty men had been subjected to sexual harassment. While the Department of

Defense had been worked on reducing such incidences in the military, she argued that the Veteran's Millennium Health Care Act would make the department more successful in that it provided the members of the military with access to sexual trauma counseling.[76]

The Senate agreed to the conference report by unanimous consent. Following the passage of the Veteran's Millennium Health Care Act - Conference Report, the bill was sent to the White House. President William Jefferson Clinton signed it into law on November 30, 1999. The president explained he signed the bill because it included measures that would enhance the implementation of veteran's compensation, housing programs, memorial affairs and the health care system.[77] While the statement he issued on the signing of VMHCA was brief, his reasoning represented a sense of indebtedness the nation has to care for veterans who risked their lives in order to protect and preserve democracy in the United States.

Hence, H.R. 2116 is significant because it expanded long-term care and nursing care. Most importantly, the Act provided medical services that had never been included in the history of veteran's entitlement programs in the United States such as primary care services, home-based care services, grant awards to state operated veteran's homes, and sexual trauma counseling.[78]

Conclusion

The House Committee on Veteran's Affairs and the Senate Committee on Veteran's Affairs played an integral role in the passage of the Veteran's Millennium Health Care Act (VMHCA) of 1999. During the first session of the 106th Congress, the bill was introduced by the House Republicans and was considered by the House Committee on Veteran's Affairs and the House Veteran's Affairs Subcommittee on Health. Republican and Democratic committee members supported the provisions outlined in the Veteran's Millennium Health Care Act and embraced provisions written by their Democratic colleagues on the committee.

Although the Democratic members were in the minority, they overwhelmingly supported the provisions included in H.R. 2116. Members supported the bill due to the fact that several of the stipulations in the House version of the bill were incorporated from legislation previously introduced by the House Veteran's Affairs

Committee ranking member, Representative Lane Evans (D-IL). The majority of Democrats voted for the VMHCA. Some voted for the bill as part of a strategy to help Democrats in the November 2000 elections. Democrats also rallied around the Act because many of its provisions were proposed by Veteran's Affairs Committee ranking member, Lane Evans (D-IL). As a measure of good faith, Democrats and Republicans, alike, joined forces to display bi-partisan cooperation. Consequently, members of the Democratic Party crossed party-lines and voted in favor of the bill. Those who opposed the bill did so because they believed the legislation failed to completely reform veteran's health care and benefits.

The Senate considered the legislation in a similar fashion. Members of the Republican Party voted along party-lines and members of the Democratic Party crossed party lines in support of the Act. Like in the House, members of both parties in the Senate supported it. In addition, the legislation represented the first effort by Congress, in over 20 years, to redress veteran's issues in a comprehensive bill. Furthermore, veteran's health care and benefits are rarely considered controversial in nature and are typically supported by the majority of members of both the Democratic and Republican Parties. The House Veteran's Affairs Subcommittee on Hospitals and Health held hearings on the Veteran's Millennium Health Care Act and the future of veteran's health care. A number of organizations including veteran's groups, state veteran's agencies and executive officials testified before the committees in an effort to express their opinion on the legislation.

Accordingly, the political environment and campaign year, the political climate, the timeliness of the legislation, and the non-controversial nature of most veteran's legislation were crucial factors in the passage of the Veteran's Millennium Health Care Act. Consequently, these factors contributed to its swift passage. The bill was introduced, passed and signed into law in a virtually unprecedented six month period.

Notes

---

[1] U.S. Congress, U.S. Congress, House Committee on Veterans Affairs, " Veterans Affairs Committee Member List," 106th Cong., 1st sess. , [database on-line] available from http://www.veterans.house.gov/about/committee.htm; Internet; accessed 5 February 2000, and U.S. Congress, House Committee on

---

Veterans Affairs Subcommittees, " Veterans Affairs Subcommittee Member List," 106th Cong., 1st sess. [database on-line] available from http://www.veterans.house.gov/about/committee/subcom.htm; Interenet; accessed 5 February 2000.

2 U.S. Congress, House, Committee on Veterans Affairs, Subcommitttee on Hospitals and Health, *Proposed Veterans Millennium Health Care Act*, H.R. 2116, 106th Congress, 1st sess., 19 May 1999.

3 U.S. Congress, House, Committee on Veterans Affairs, Subcommittee on Hospitals and Health, *The Veterans Millennium Health Care Act*, H.R. 2116 – Markup, 106th Cong., 1st sess., 9 June 1999.

4 U.S. Congress, House Committee on Veterans Affairs, " Veterans Affairs Committee Member List," 106th Cong., 1st sess. , [database on-line] available from http://www.veterans.house.gov/about/committee.htm; Internet; accessed 5 February 2000, and U.S. Congress, House Committee on Veterans Affairs Subcommittees, " Veterans Affairs Subcommittee Member List," 106th Cong., 1st sess. [database on-line] available from http://www.veterans.house.gov/about/committee/subcom.htm; Interenet; accessed 5 February 2000.

5 Ibid.

6 Ibid.

7 Ibid.

8 Ibid.

9 U.S. Congress, House, Committee on Veterans Affairs, *The Veterans Millennium Health Care Act*, 106th Cong., 1st sess., 9 June 1999.

10 U.S. Congress, House, Committee on Veterans Affairs, Subcommittee on Hospitals and Health, *Cost Estimates for the Veterans Millennium Health Care Act*, H.R. 2116, Report by Paul Van de Water, 106th Cong., 1st sess., 30 June 1999.

11 Ibid., 1-3.

12 Ibid., 10.

[13] Ibid.

[14] Ibid., 7-8.

[15] Ibid., 9.

[16] Ibid., 9-10.

[17] Ibid.

[18] Ibid., 11.

[19] Ibid.

[20] Ibid., 12.

[21] Ibid.

[22] Ibid., 14.

[23] U.S. Congress, House, Committee on Veterans Affairs, Subcommittee on Benefits, *Hearing on H.R. 605, H.R. 690, H.R. 784, H.R. 1212, and H.R. 1765*, H.R. 474, 106th Cong., 1st sess., 10 June 1999.

[24] U.S. Congress, House, Committee on Veterans Affairs, Subcommittee on Benefits, *Hearing on H.R. 605, H.R. 690, H.R. 784, H.R. 1212, and H.R. 1765*, H.R. 1214, 106th Cong., 1st sess., 10 June 1999.

[25] U.S. Congress, House, Committee on Veterans Affairs, Subcommittee on Benefits, *Hearing on H.R. 1247, H.R. 1476, H.R. 1484, H.R. 1603, H.R. 1663, H.R. 1247,* 106th Cong., 1st sess., 16 June 1999.

[26] U.S. Congress, House, Committee on Veterans Affairs, Subcommittee on Benefits, *Hearing on H.R. 1247, H.R. 1476, H.R. 1484, H.R. 1603, H.R. 1663,* H.R. 1633, 106th Cong., 1st sess., 16 June 1999.

[27] U.S. Congress, House, Committee on Veterans Affairs, Subcommittee on Benefits, *Hearing on H.R. 1247, H.R. 1476, H.R. 1484, H.R. 1603, H.R. 1663,* H.R. 1476, 106th Cong., 1st sess., 16 June 1999.

---

[28] U.S. Congress, House, Committee on Veterans Affairs, Subcommittee on Benefits, *Hearing on H.R. 605, H.R. 690, H.R. 784, H.R. 1212, and H.R. 1765*, H.R. 784, 106th Cong., 1st sess., 10 June 1999.

[29] U.S. Congress, House, Committee on Veterans Affairs, *The Veterans Millennium Health Care Act*, H.R. 2116, 106th Cong., 1st sess., 15 June 1999.

[30] Ibid.

[31] U.S. Congress, House, Representative Cliff Stearns of Florida speaking for the Veterans Millennium Health Care Act, H.R. 2116, 106th Cong., 1st sess., *Congressional Record* (3 August 1999), vol. 145, H6945.

[32] Ibid.

[33] Ibid.

[34] U.S. Congress, House, Representative Bob Filner of California speaking for the Veterans Millennium Health Care Act, H.R. 2116, 106th Cong., 1st sess., *Congressional Record* 145 (5 August 1999), no. 114, E1784.

[35] Ibid.

[36] Ibid.

[37] U.S. Congress, House, Committee on Veterans Affairs, "The Veterans Millennium Health Care Act", Roll Call Vote 427, 106th Cong., 1st sess., *Congressional Record* (21 September 1999) [database on-line] available from http://clerkweb.house.gov/cgi-bin/vote.exe?year=1999&rollnumber=427; Internet; accessed 5 July 2000.

[38] U.S. Congress, House, Representative Eva Clayton of North Carolina speaking for the Veterans Millennium Health Care Act, H.R. 2116, 106th Cong., *Congressional Record* 145 (23 September 1999), no. 125, E1947.

[39] U.S. Congress, House, Representative Steny Hoyer of Maryland speaking for the Veterans Millennium Health Care Act, H.R. 2116, 106th Cong., 1st sess., *Congressional Record* 145 (4 October 1999), no. 133, E2023.

[40] Ibid.

[41] U.S Congress, House, Representative Harold Rogers of Kentucky speaking for the Veterans Millennium Health Care Act, H.R. 2116, 106th Cong., 1st sess., *Congressional Record* 145 (24 September 1999), no. 126, E1956.

[42] U.S. Congress, House Representative Ron Packard of California speaking for the Veterans Millennium Health Care Act, H.R. 2116, 106th Cong., 1st sess., *Congressional Record* 145 (22 September 1999), no. 124, E1922.

[43] U.S. Congress, Senate, Committee on Veterans Affairs, "Veterans Affairs Member List," 106th Cong., 1st sess., [database on-line] available from http://www.senate.gov/committees; Internet; acessed 5 February 2000.

[44] U.S. Congress, Senate, Committee on Veterans Affairs, *The Veterans Millennium Health Care Act*, S. AMDT 2541, 106th Cong., 1st sess., 5 November1999.

[45] Ibid.

[46] Ibid, 5-8.

[47] U.S. Congress, Senate, Senator John Rockefeller of West Virginia speaking for the Veterans Millennium Health Care Act Conference Report, H.R. 2116, 106th Cong., 1st sess., *Congressional Record* 145 (19 November 1999), no. 165, S14905.

[48] U.S. Congress, Senate, Senator Pete Domenici of New Mexico speaking for the Veterans Millennium Health Care Act Conference Report, H.R. 2116, 106th Cong., 1st sess., *Congressional Record* 145 (19 November 1999), no. 125, S14905.

[49] U.S. Congress, Senate, Senator John Rockefeller of West Virginia speaking for the Veterans Millennium Health Care Act Conference Report, H.R. 2116, 106th Cong., 1st sess., *Congressional Record* 145 (19 November 1999), no. 165, S 14909.

[50] U.S. Congress, Senate, Senator Olympia Snowe of Maine speaking for the Veterans Millennium Health Care Act Conference Report, H.R. 2116, 106th Cong., 1st sess., *Congressional Record* 145 (19 November 1999), no. 165, S14909.

---

[51] U.S. Congress, Senate, Senator John Rockefeller of West Virginia speaking for the Veterans Millennium Health Care Act Conference Report, H.R. 2116, 106th Cong., 1st sess., *Congressional Record* 145 (19 November 1999), no. 165, S14905.

[52] U.S. Congress, House, "Appointment of Conferees for "Veterans Millennium Health Care Act," 106th Cong., 1st sess., *Congressional Research Service* 145 (8 November 1999), no. 164, H11678.

[53] For a listing of the members of the 106th Congress who served in the U.S. Military a chart listing names, ranks, dates of service, and information on members service in combat is available in my dissertation "A Study of the Veteran's Millennium Health Care and Benefits Act of 1999" accepted by Howard University in 2002. The dissertation is available through Proquest/UMI. Information can also be retrieved from the House Veteran's Affairs Committee homepage at http://veterans.house/vetcong/vetcong.htm.

[54] Stanley Bach, "Instructing House Conferees," *Congresional Research Service,* [database on-line] available from http://www.house.gov/riles/98-381.htm; Internet; accessed 5 July 2000., 1.

[55] Ibid.

[56] James Saturno, "Floor Consideration of Conference Reports in the House," *Congressional Research Service,* [database on-line] available from http://www.house.gov/rules/98-736.htm; Internet; accessed 5 July 2000, 1.

[57] Ibid.

[58] Ibid., 1-2.

[59] Ibid.

[60] U.S. Congress, House, Representative Sheila Jackson-Lee of Texas speaking for the Veterans Millennium Health Care Act Conference Report, H.R. 2116, 106th Cong., 1st sess., *Congressional Record* 145 (16 November 1999), no. 164, E2435.

[61] Ibid.

---

[62] Ibid.

[63] U.S. Congress, House, Representative Michael Doyle of Pennsylvania speaking for the Veterans Millennium Health Care Act, H.R. 2116, 106th Cong., 1st sess., *Congressional Record* 145 (16 November 1999), no. 162, E2453.

[64] U.S. Congress, House, Representative Christopher Smith of New Jersey speaking for the Veterans Millennium Health Care Act, H.R. 2116, 106th Cong., 1st sess., *Congressional Record* 145 (16 November 1999), no. 162, E2531.

[65] Ibid.

[66] Ibid.

[67] Ibid.

[68] U.S. Congress, Senate, Senator Arlen Specter of Pennsylvania speaking for the Veterans Millennium Health Care Act, H.R. 2116, 196th Cong., 1st sess., *Congressional Record* 145 (19 November 1999), no. 165, S14904.

[69] Ibid.

[70] Ibid.

[71] Ibid.

[72] U.S. Congress, Senate, Senator Pete Domenici of New Mexico speaking for the Veterans Millennium Health Care Act Conference Report, H.R. 2116, 106th Cong., 1st sess., *Congressional Record* 145 (19 November 1999), no. 125, S14904.

[73] U.S. Congress, Senate, Senator John Rockefeller of West Virginia speaking for the Veterans Millennium Health Care Act Conference Repor, H.R. 2116, 106th Cong., 1st sess., *Congressional Record* 145 (19 November 1999), no. 165, S14905.

[74] Ibid.

[75] U.S. Congress, Senate, Senator Olympia Snowe of Maine speaking for the Veterans Millennium Health Care Act Confernce Report, H.R. 2116, 106th Cong., 1st sess., *Congressional Record* 145 (19 November 1999), no. 165, S14905.

[76] Ibid.

[77] U.S. President William Clinton, Proclamation, "On Signing the Veterans Millennium Health Care Benefits Act," Federal Register 64 (30 November 1999), no. 2, 2473.

[78] Ibid.

CHAPTER 4

PUBLIC OPINION AND PRESSURE GROUPS

This chapter explores the role of public opinion and interest groups behavior in influencing the Veteran's Millennium Health Care Act (VMHCA) of 1999. It examines the impact of public opinion on the bi-partisan veteran's bill. This chapter also treats the role of the veteran's lobby is observed through a discussion of the activities employed by various veteran's organizations.

Public Opinion and Veteran's Benefits

Public opinion is particularly valuable because it is an expression of the attitudes, values and beliefs held by individuals. Public opinion also is useful when issues or policies are widely embraced by citizens or there is homogeneity of popular opinion in a nation. Public opinion can add to the value of citizenship in that people feel a sense of value and belonging in a nation. Public opinion and attitudes held by others have the ability to influence the opinions articulated by others.

The history and magnitude of veteran's entitlements, i.e. medical care, loan programs, disability pension, etc., suggests a prevalent sense of responsibility for the well-being of veterans in the United States. The evolution of veteran's entitlements is treated in

Chapter One. The general public opinion that existed in the early to mid- 1900s was that the nation needed to increase government assistance to veterans. In 1947, less than one year before the enactment of The Disabled Veteran's Rehabilitation Act,[1] an attempt to measure public opinion on the adequacy of veteran's benefits was conducted. Participants of the survey were asked whether the federal government provided veterans with adequate benefits. The response was that veteran's benefits were insufficient.[2] During that same period, the Gallup organization conducted another survey on public opinion about veteran's benefits. The organization asked adults whether veterans were receiving adequate benefits. Fifty-three percent (53%) of respondents indicated that benefits were adequate. However, thirty-two percent (32%) of respondents maintained that veteran's benefits were inadequate.[3]

During the 1950s, public opinion was almost evenly split over whether the federal government should provide "free" medical care to veterans if they were not injured in combat. Forty-nine percent of respondents, in a 1953 poll conducted by the Gallup organization, opposed giving free medical treatment to veterans whose injuries were not related to their service in the military. However, forty-five percent of participants believed the government should provide free treatment irrespective of when veterans sustained their injuries.[4]

In an effort to determine how the public felt towards veterans, the Veteran's Administration conducted a survey from November through December 1979. The data suggested that the American public overwhelmingly supported veterans. Participants were asked to describe their regard for veterans on a scale of 1% through 10%; a 1% represented low regard while a 10% represented the highest possible regard. When asked to describe how they felt about Prisoners of War (POWs) captured in Vietnam, the data (median score of 10) shows the high regard for POWs. Participants also expressed a great respect for veterans who served in Vietnam. Their fondness for these veterans ranked at 9.8%. The survey data also recorded a sentiment of appreciation for the sacrifices of World War II and Korean War veterans; they registered as 9.6%. A slightly lower level (8.7%) of fondness was expressed for veterans who served in the military.

In addition, Louis Harris and Associates conducted a survey of public opinion on veteran's entitlements. They asked adults in the national population to answer a series of questions on veteran's benefits. Respondents were instructed to respond to the questions by indicating more help, less help, treat like other groups, not sure. When asked whether the government should provide increased assistance to emotionally or psychologically disturbed Vietnam veterans, 66% indicated that the government should give these veterans additional assistance. Thirty-one percent (31%), however, stated that they should be treated like other groups.[5]

That same year, public opinion was supportive of veteran's benefits. The Veteran's administration sponsored a survey to determine the level of public support for various benefits offered to veterans. Eighty-six percent (86%) favored providing health care to veterans, especially Vietnam veterans.[6] The majority of people interviewed strongly encouraged (83%) the government to guarantee home loans for veterans.[7] Seventy-seven percent (77%) of respondents favored the federal government providing career counseling for veterans.[8]

Additionally, *ABC News and Louis Harris and Associates* jointly conducted a survey to determine what serious problems the public believed plagued the veterans community. Among the top responses were (1) psychological health issues (39%), (2) Employment issues (38%), and (3) drug and alcohol addiction (24%). Another twelve percent (12%) of the participants identified health issues as a major concern facing America's veterans. It is important to note that the survey utilized an open-ended question. This allowed respondents to answer the question based on their knowledge of veteran's issues.[9]

Consequently, a *Gallup Poll* was used to follow up with the respondents discussed in the previous survey. They were specifically asked, "What should they (veterans) get that they are not now getting (for benefits)?" Forty-five percent (45%) stated that veterans should receive more money. Thirty percent (30%) indicated that veterans should receive homes. Despite the relatively small percentages in other categories (less than 10%), public opinion also suggested that the government should consider giving veterans preference in employment, increase educational benefits, and improve their medical care. Generally, the sentiment of public opinion indicated that people believed the government was not sufficiently providing for those who fought in war.[10]

In 1984, President Reagan considered cutting domestic social programs in order to increase federal defense spending. *Louis Harris and Associates* conducted a survey to measure public support for the president's proposal. The polling data suggested that the public did not support President's proposal to reduce spending on domestic social programs. In fact, none of those interviewed supported the proposal. However, sixty-nine percent (69%) said they would support cutting defense spending. Another eighteen percent (18%) preferred that the president look at reducing expenditures in other federal programs as an alternative to cutting domestic social programs.[11]

Public opinion in the 1980s heavily opposed changing the frequency at which cost-of-living adjustments (COLAs) were distributed to veterans and surviving spouses. In 1985, the House and Senate Budget Committees considered creating a new system of implementing veteran's benefits. A poll was conducted by *Louis Harris and Associates* to determine public opinion on the Budget Committees' proposal. Adults from the national population were interviewed and asked whether the government should go to a new system under which veterans beneficiaries and social security recipients would receive their cost-of-living increases every year rather than every other year as previously practiced. The majority of those interviewed (56%) opposed changing the entitlement programs. In comparison, forty-three percent (43%) of the respondents favored the proposal.[12]

In 1986, public opinion suggested that only twenty-nine percent (29%) favored cutting federal spending on entitlement programs like veterans, social security, and welfare benefits.[13] While only twenty-nine percent (29%) of those interviewed supported reducing government spending was minor, one can surmise that the percentage might have been smaller had welfare not been included in veterans and social security remuneration. Furthermore, more than half (53%) of those interviewed shared the sentiment that defense spending should be reduced. Consequently, public opinion in the United States on veterans, social security and Medicare was favorable.

During the 1990 budget debates between President George Bush, Sr. and Congress, public opinion opposed the president's proposal to cut entitlement programs in order to reduce the national deficit. The majority of those interviewed indicated that they favored the position of the Democratic Party to find another alternative to reduce the deficit. More than 1,200 adults were randomly selected from the national population. The majority of participants opposed President George Bush proposal to reduce spending on entitlement programs like veteran's benefits. Fifty-three percent (53%) of the respondents supported the Democratic position on the issue, while forty-four percent (44%) supported the president's position.[14]

In a 1991 survey sponsored by the National Organization on Disability, eighty-nine percent (89%) of the respondents supported veterans programs, Medicare, and Social Security. Of those who favored these entitlements, forty-three percent (43%) strongly supported the programs, while forty-six percent (46%) were moderately supportive.[15]

The Kaiser Foundation and Harvard School of Public Health sponsored a survey to measure public opinion on a proposal to reduce spending on veteran's benefits. The data suggested that the public opposed the plan. This is substantiated by the fact that seventy-seven percent (77%) of the participants opposed reducing spending on veterans programs. Only a small percentage of twenty-one percent (21%) favored doing so.[16]

By 1996, political leaders were focusing on ways to reduce the Consumer Price Index. One proposal considered by government leaders suggested reducing the amount veterans and social security beneficiaries received as cost-of-living increases. Although, controversial, the plan would have helped reduce the national deficit. *NBC News and Wall Street Journal* sponsored the survey and asked people "Do you favor reducing the Consumer Price Index in this manner. Forty-seven percent (47%) of those interviewed supported decreasing the amount of cost-of-living increases given to veterans and disabled individuals to offset inflation. However, forty-three percent (43%) of the participants disagreed with the proposed plan; 23 % strongly opposed the plan and 20% somewhat opposed the proposal.[17] The responses suggest that participants in the survey had reservations about the impact such a plan would have on veterans. Perhaps, if given another alternative to reducing the deficit, these respondents would have opposed diminishing veterans cost-of-living adjustment (COLA). This sentiment is based on public opinion expressed in a survey conducted by the *Los Angeles Times* in 1996. Those interviewed were asked whether presidential candidate Bob Dole's plan to cut income taxes by 15 percent, reduce capital gains taxes and give a $500 per child tax credit could be achieved. The majority of respondents (60%) believed the proposed plan was impractical and unrealistic.[18]

The Employee Benefit Institute was interested in the public's confidence in income retirement programs. Therefore, it conducted a survey to measure public confidence in these programs. The institute defined a retirement plan as money provided by either an employer or employee that is set-aside for a 401K or personal savings account. The definition also included government income programs like Social Security Income and veteran's benefits. Twenty-six percent (26%) of the respondents shared the belief that personal retirement accounts would be their most important source of retirement income. Another, twenty-two percent (22%) expressed confidence in relying on income retirement programs provided by their employer. Some indicated that they felt comfortable their personal savings would be sufficient. A small percentage (18%) also noted a belief that social security would be their primary source of retirement income. However, shamefully none (0%) of the respondents expressed confidence in veteran's benefits as a source of retirement income.[19] Consequently, it became apparent that public opinion does not support the idea that veterans programs are adequate retirement income sources. Thus, public opinion data suggest that Americans favor expanding veteran's benefits and improving the delivery of health care services.

Interest Groups and the Passage of the Veterans Millennium Health Care Act

There exists a wealth of literature in the area of interest group behavior. This chapter discusses the role of interest groups and interest group activities in the shaping and passage of the 1999 veteran's legislation. This chapter highlights the scholarly literature of Arthur Bentley, *The Process of Government*, David Truman, *The Government Process*, Jeffrey Berry, *The Interest Group Society* and *Lobbying for the People,* and James Madison's *Federalist Paper* No. 10. In addition this exposition covers theories and concepts developed in the literature of V. O. Key, *Politics, Parties and Pressure Groups*, and Abraham Holtzman, *Interest Groups and Lobbying.*

James Madison's paper *Federalist #10* marks the first discussion of pressure groups and their potential impact on American society. James Madison defined the concept of "factions" as a group of individuals who are spurred into action by a shared objective or interest. He contends that the virtues and vices associated with these groups lie in their ability to influence the government to promote their interest. Madison postulated that the evils associated with factions are rooted in human nature or the natural state of man. That being so, a representative form of government would be best since it would allow for a "collage" of interests to be attended. As such, he believes urges that the influence of factions will be limited since all of them will have an equal chance of influencing the government.[20] In more contemporary times, factions are referred to as either interest groups or pressure groups.

Jeffrey M. Berry in his book *The Interest Group Society* defines interest groups as a collection of people that unite for the sole purpose of influencing public policy outcomes. He explains that these groups form for "issue-oriented" reasons. They are simply "channels through which politically concerned people direct their time, money, and psychological involvement. Thus, Berry argues that interest groups serve as a means by which people collectively participate in politics.[21]

In *Lobbying for the People*, Jeffrey Berry defines a "public interest" as "one that seeks a collective good, the achievement of which will not selectively and materially benefit the membership or activists of the organization."[22] Moreover, Jeffrey Berry in *Lobbying for the People*, asserted that monitoring programs are beneficial to interest groups because they occasionally decide to publicly endorse government officials, inspire letter writing campaigns or make financial contributions to government officials.[23] The author discusses the various tactics and strategies employed by interest groups; these strategies are used to influence governmental institutions, i.e., executive and legislature, etc.... He stresses interest groups participate in (1) political protests, (2) whistle-blowing, (3) conducting research studies, (4) lobbying, (5) letter-writing campaigns and (6) testifying at congressional hearings.[24]

Likewise, Abraham Holtzman's book *Interest Groups and Lobbying* observes that interest groups are instruments "through which individuals and group units of power can be maximized to influence government."[25] In his article "The Origins and Maintenance of Interest Groups in America," Walker suggests that the maintenance of groups depend on the group's ability to secure funding. He notes that organizations participate in collecting membership dues, magazine or journal subscriptions, as well as contributions from the private sector; interest groups depend heavily on both internal and external financial support.[26]

Arthur Bentley's book *The Process of Government* significantly contributes to the field of American Government, particularly interest group activities. The author defines interest groups as a particular portion of men of a society who participate in society through taking part in group activities. He argues that in order for a group to exist, it must have common or core interests. The activities of a group are based on the sentiment and ideas of individual members of the group. Thus, individuals unite in pursuit of shared objectives, goals and beliefs. The formulation of a group is crucial because the ability to apply pressure is a group phenomenon. The application of pressure in the political system forces compromise within the system. Consequently, much of American government operates within a process of negotiation.[27]

Bentley maintains that interest groups encounter varying degrees of resistance to their claims in both the legislative and executive branches of government. Consequently, interest groups sometimes opt to primarily apply pressure to either Congress or the White House. The decision to primarily focus on one branch of government is determined by how receptive either has been to a group's public policy interests.[28]

David Truman in *The Governmental Process* expands on Bentley's work. He defines an interest group as one that makes claims upon other groups in the society in an effort to formulate, implement, maintain and enhance the behavior of the decision-makers based on the shared attitudes of group members. He notes that tendency to join groups is innate to the very nature of man. Truman argues that groups are an intricate part of the American political system because they are closely related to the daily functions and operation of the political process. As such, the political process cannot be adequately treated without discussing aspects of interest groups.[29] Apart from the proceeding, Truman discusses the ability of a group to gain access to governmental institutions. He notes that a group's effectiveness in gaining access to government institutions greatly depends on the group's position in society. Moreover, its internal characteristics and the manner in which a group attempts to relate to governmental institutes determine the effectiveness of a group.[30]

Jeffrey Berry, in his seminal work *The Interest Group Society,* defines an interest group as "an organized body of individuals who share similar goals or values and try to influence policy out comes."[31] An attempt by an interest group to apply pressure or influence policymakers is referred to as lobbying. Lobbying can be aimed directly at a particular governmental institution, (i.e., legislature, judicial or executive). However, interest groups are also apt to indirectly influence institutions through swaying public opinion in an effort to influence government and the direction of public policy.[32]

Berry maintains that interest groups are significant in American society due to their membership. Furthermore, interest groups represent the views of larger constituencies.[33]

In addition, Jeffrey Berry highlights the different roles of interest groups. He observes that interest groups play four primary roles in American politics. Interest groups provide people the opportunity to participate in the political process. Individual members can contribute monetary donations to lobbying organizations, write letters to members of Congress and participate in protests. These activities facilitate participation in interest groups. Furthermore, interest groups actively promote participation in the legislative process by stimulating its members to act on behalf of a particular cause. Second, interest groups act in an effort to represent their members and constituents before government officials by educating members of Congress and the American public about political issues. Moreover, interest groups educate people through publications, publicity campaigns and proposed recommendations or solutions.[34]

V.O. Key categorizes interests on the basis of their ideology: (1) agrarian, (2) labor, (3) business, and (4) other - religious, veterans, and racial minorities. He maintains that the agrarian ideology advocates support for farmers.[35] Labor groups urge the government to extend fiscal policies, which have been greatly diminished by price controls and minimum wage requirements.[36] Key states that the business lobby embraces an ideology built upon a competitive free-market with the government having a minor role.[37] The final category encompasses veterans, religious organizations, and minorities, particularly "Negroes." The author says these groups act as "ad hoc" organizations. Their primary goal is to advocate on behalf of or against public policy proposals. According to him, ad hoc groups coordinate or pool their efforts with other organizations to form alliances; through coordinated efforts, veteran's groups and minorities can strengthen their political influence.[38]

Interest groups also participate in agenda building and educating people about the different perspectives of an issue. Agenda building serves as a means by which problems are transformed into issues. Finally, interest groups are involved in monitoring programs. They follow programs that affect their membership by bringing attention to issues through use of evaluative reports and contacts with the media. In addition, they lobby agency or department personnel in an attempt to bring about changes in program implementation.[39]

On occasion, interest groups or interests that fail to be placed on the agenda of the legislative and executive branches of government occasionally utilized the judiciary as an entry point to redress public policy wrongs. Hanes Walton's *Black Politics* substantiates this claim by illustrating how successful this tactic became during the Civil Rights Movement for African-Americans when Congress and the Chief Executive failed to handle the issue of segregation.[40] Thus, the National Association of Colored People (NAACP) turned to the judiciary as a means of redressing segregation laws that the organization viewed as unconstitutional.

Similarly, Jeffrey Berry notes that pressure groups occasionally utilize litigation as a strategy to prompt the government to enact public policy. Organizations like the Sierra Club and Common Cause consider litigation to be another means of advocacy.[41] Veteran's interest groups, i.e. The Retired Officers Association (TREA), Paralyzed Veterans of America (PVA), the National Commissioned Officers Association (NCOA), The American Legion, etc., use litigation as an alternative strategy. When these groups use suits as a means of advocacy, they tend to fair poorly in administrative or legislative courts. On the other hand, advocacy groups fair more favorably in federal court. This is largely because administrative courts act as loyal subunits of government. Thus, advocacy groups such as veteran's organizations view these courts as hostile. Furthermore, the courts have not always agreed with the way interest groups interpret the law. Nevertheless, when all else fails, interest groups and lobbyists continue to seek redress in the courts.[42]

In *Politics, Parties and Pressure Groups*, V.O. Key addresses veteran's organizations as interest groups. He argues that following war; veterans placed large amounts of pressure on the government for assistance programs. Therefore, the "soldier" has been "set apart from the civilian and undoubtedly cement such groups together."[43] He surmises that the preoccupation of veterans with pensions, bonuses, and other benefits has become a "conspicuous" characteristic.[44]

One of the most influential veteran's organizations is the American Legion. It was formed following World War I. Soon thereafter, the group's membership reached 1,000,000. By 1950, the Legion reached a membership of more than 3,000,000.[45] The veteran's organization now boasts a membership of 2,5000,000.

The American Legion does not nominate or endorse candidates for public office because its constitution stipulates that:

"The American Legion shall be absolutely non-political and shall not be used for the dissemination of partisan principles nor for the promotion of the candidacy of any persons seeking public office or preferment. No candidate for or incumbent of a salaried elective public office shall hold any office in the American Legion or in a Department or Post thereof."[46]

However, the Legion does have the freedom to articulate its public policy goals. The non-partisan nature of the veteran's organization "prevents division" and maintains group unity.[47]

V.O. Key, further, argues that "war veterans", especially those disabled in battle, have a special claim" on the country. The sense of indebtedness a country feels for its veterans create a favorable environment for the legislative agendas pushed by these groups. It is especially noteworthy to mention that veteran's organizations like the American Legion do not contend with opposition from other pressure groups.[48]

Despite favorable conditions, veteran's groups leave no stone unturned. They compile and disseminate voting records on members of Congress on issues of particular interest to them. Much of the organization's strength comes from grassroots lobbying. Similarly, veteran's groups that represent disabled veterans like the Paralyzed Veterans of America also have long standing. Disabled veteran's groups have a limited membership base in comparison to the American Legion; this is because these groups represent veterans with disabilities incurred during military service. In fact, this particular membership requirement adds strength to demands for special entitlements, i.e., medical services, pension, loans, education, etc.... Other veteran's interest groups include Veterans of Foreign Wars (VFW), Non-Commissioned Officers Association (NCOA), The Retired Enlisted Officers Association, and the Vietnam Veterans of America (VVA).[49] These veteran's pressure groups and others rallied around the expansion of veteran's entitlements included in H.R. 2116 - the Veteran's Millennium Health Care Act (VMHCA) of 1999, and thereby contributed to its enactment by the 106th Congress.

These groups maintained communication with members of Congress and the White House through use of mailings, phone calls, face-to-face meetings, and testifying at committee hearings on veteran's issues such as respite care, nursing home care, and long-term medical treatment options. Veteran's pressure groups heavily participated in the "Veterans Annual Legislative Hearings" held by the House and Senate Veteran's Affairs Committees. These hearings allowed veteran's interest groups to pinpoint issue areas that they believed needed to be addressed by Congress and the Executive Branch -- the Department of Veteran's Affairs. According to Steve Robertson, Legislative Director for the American Legion, the group drafted the original language in House bill H.R. 2116. However, the final bill differed greatly from the original language drafted by the veteran's interest group.[50] Representative Cliff Stearns (R-FL) sponsored the legislation.

Veteran's groups, i.e. Paralyzed Veterans of American (PVA), Jewish War Veterans (JWV), Vietnam Veterans of America (VVA), Non-Commissioned Officers Association (NCOA), State Veterans Homes Association, American Health Care Association (AHCA), also joined to impress upon Congress the need for legislation to reform veteran's medical care and benefits. Although the veteran's groups represent different memberships, their mission focuses on improving the lives of America's veterans and their dependents. Although each of the veteran's organizations has special needs determined by its membership, they articulated very similar legislative agendas.

Prior to the drafting of H. R. 2116 - The Veteran's Millennium Health Care Act (VMHCA), the House and Senate Committee on Veteran's affairs conducted a hearing on "The Impact of Budget Shortfalls on the Delivery of Health Care to Rural Veterans." On December 2, 1908, A.V. Aiken of the American Legion testified on the impact of budget shortfalls on the delivery of health care services for veterans living in rural areas. The American Legion argued that the budget freeze the Veteran's administration experienced adversely affected veterans who received inpatient and outpatient care in medical facilities administered by the Veteran's administration (VA). The organization argued that the lack of adequate funding in the Department of Veteran's Affairs budget in the early 1980's led to the closing of approximately 20 medical facilities managed by the Veteran's administration (VA). This compelled veterans to endure a lot of suffering. For example, the American Legion noted that the closure of medical facilities forced many veterans to travel long distances outside of their communities to obtain medical treatment at veteran's facilities in other counties and cities. Moreover, Aiken asserted that the closures placed an undue burden on veterans, many of who could not afford to finance an additional travel expenses incurred in their pursuit of obtaining medical treatment. The organization noted that the budget shortfalls eroded "the quality, quantity and timeliness of health care services provided" to its constituents, membership and United States veterans alike. [51] Finally, the American Legion argued that budget shortfalls adversely impacted veterans. Therefore, the organization asserted that such shortfalls needed to be remedied in a manner that reflected "the just dues of the men and women... that answered the call of the elected Government to defend the national interest in the Armed Forces."[52]

During the first session of 106th Congress, numerous groups were instrumental in the passage of the "Veterans Millennium Health Care Act" of 1999. Many of the influential organizations that stressed the significance of the Act were interest groups that represented veterans, state and local agencies, and medical professionals, all of whom highlighted inefficiencies, inadequacies, and a lack of access to medical treatment in the veteran's health care system. In response to the state of veteran's health care in the United States, specifically the administration of the VA health care system, veteran's organizations mobilized themselves and employed various strategies in an attempt to influence the legislative and executive branches of government on the comprehensive 1999 veteran's health care and benefits legislation. Veteran's groups, state and local agency administrators and medical professionals were among some of the principal groups that influenced the formulation and passage of the veteran's legislation. These groups disseminated information to veterans and caregivers about the condition of veteran's health care. They also wrote letters to members of Congress, and testified at congressional hearings held by the House and Senate Committees on Veteran's Affairs.

The Activities and Testimony of Veteran's Interest Groups

The House and Senate Veteran's Affairs Committee held joint annual hearings that afforded veteran's organization's opportunities to discuss their views on veteran's issues. These annual hearings provided them the opportunity to contribute towards addressing crucial issues that affected their constituencies. Groups such as the Veterans of Foreign Wars of the United States (VFW), Jewish War Veterans (JWV) and Non-Commissioned Officers Association of the United States of America (NCOA) were extended the opportunity to provide insight on issues pertaining to veteran's health care and benefits (e.g., education, health, housing, pension, etc...).[53] On March 2, 1999, the House of Representatives and Senate Veteran's Affairs Committees held a joint committee hearing. This joint committee hearing was part of an annual legislative presentation in which veteran's organizations provided Congress with information about the variety of veteran's health concerns.[54] A number of veteran's interest groups participated in the annual hearing. For example, Thomas A. Pouliot, the Commander-in-Chief of the Veterans of Foreign Wars of the United States (the VFW composed of soldiers, sailors, airman, Coastguardsmen and Marines who fought in wars to protect the united States interests abroad. In short, the Veterans of Foreign Wars (VFW) advocated on behalf of its members in an effort to ensure the protection and expansion of veteran's entitlements and benefit programs.[55]

Pouliot shared the views of the VFW on the budget surplus and the President's fiscal year 2000 Veteran's Administration (VA) Budget. He noted that while numerous programs were slated to receive large increases in their budget, veteran's programs and initiatives appeared to have been overlooked again. In addition, he asserted that the Clinton administration seemed "intent on leaving veterans out in the cold." Consequently, he maintained that it was the responsibility of members of the House and Senate Veteran's Affairs Committees to take a leadership role to ensure that veterans were provided the care they deserve. Pouliot added that Congress ought to demonstrate its intention by expanding the VA programs and increasing funding for the Department of Veteran's Affairs.[56]

The Commander-in-Chief of the VFW asserted his belief that it was unexplainable to find American war veterans in the most vulnerable state at a time in which the country was experiencing its greatest economic prosperity in its history. Pouliot noted that funding for veteran's medical care and other benefit programs was virtually frozen at the same level for three consecutive years. He stated that chronic under-funding had essentially caused the deterioration of the Department of Veteran's Affairs' ability to provide for the needs of America's veterans. Even though, Thomas Pouliot continued President Clinton's medical care funding recommendation of $17.3 billion was an increase, it was $3 billion less than the amount requested by the Veterans of Foreign Wars (VFW). The shortage would make it impossible for the department to adequately care for veterans enrolled in the VA health care system. Consequently, the group projected that many of the medical conditions plaguing veterans would continue to deteriorate if the president's funding recommendation was implemented.[57]

Furthermore, Pouliot informed Congress that the length of time veterans spent waiting to receive treatment in specialty clinics had increased. The same was true in getting their prescription drugs filled at pharmacies in VA facilities. In addition, several veteran's organizations discovered that the number of available nursing home beds was being reduced at a time when veterans needed them most. Pouliot emphasized that these consequences were just a few of those that veterans reported to the organization's 1-800 Help Line. Finally, he declared that the alarming and tragic consequences of inadequate funding must be addressed.[58]

The Veterans of Foreign Wars urged Congress to enact legislation that would authorize the Veteran's Administration (VA) to receive and retain Medicare dollars for medical treatment provided by the VA to veterans that were eligible to participate in the Medicare program. Pouliot stressed that Medicare subvention for VA would allow more veterans to have increased access to expanded health care services. In addition, he claimed that the VA's cost-effective approach to veteran's health care services would enable the Medicare Trust Fund to save money in the process.[59]

Another critical issue discussed by the VFW during the congressional hearings was the need for expanded and improved long-term health care services. Pouliot stressed that aging veterans need intensive long-term medical treatment. He asserted that the Veterans of Foreign Wars (VFW) were in favor of legislation that would enable the VA to provide for the long-term needs of the aging veteran's population. The organization argued that expanded long-term care should include nursing home care, mental health counseling services for veterans suffering from chronic mental illness, as well as home-care assistance and support services.[60]

The Veterans of Foreign Wars (VFW) expressed concern regarding the inadequate services the Department of Veteran's Affairs Benefits Administration (VBA) provided to veterans. The organization defended its belief that the President's budget proposal failed to provide sufficient monetary resources. Pouliot highlighted the fact that the average processing time for the initial benefit claim of veterans was 160 days – more than five months. In addition, he asserted that at least 36 percent of the claims filed by veterans were adjudicated incorrectly.

Consequently, veterans who were in dire need of medical treatment were delayed and often denied the financial assistance they needed to facilitate necessary medical treatment.[61]

Nevertheless, the VFW credited the president's recommendation that the Veteran's Benefits Administration (VBA) be provided 440 additional employees for claims processing so as to expedite matters. However, the group noted that only 164 of the 440 employees would be new employees. The remaining 276 were to be taken from other areas in the Veteran's Administration. Furthermore, Pouliot argued, it would take close to three to five years to adequately train the VA employees who would be transferred from different division in the department to perform the task of claims adjudicators. Finally, the VFW argued that the fiscal year 2000 VA budget funding was $39 million below what the organization believed was necessary to implement claims processing in an effective manner.[62]

Following the group's presentation, the Veterans of Foreign Wars (VFW) hosted its annual Washington Conference Banquet on March 2, 1999. The group honored Senator Arlen Specter (R-PA), Chairman of the Senate Veteran's Affairs Committee, with its 35th Annual VFW Congressional Award citing his distinguished record of accomplishments on behalf of America's Veterans. The banquet provided the organization with yet another opportunity to attempt to influence Senator Arlen Specter, and other members of the Senate Veteran's Affairs Committee and House Veteran's Affairs Committee.

The Jewish War Veterans (JWV) also appeared before the House and Senate Joint Veteran's Affairs Committee hearing on veteran's issues, on March 4, 1999. Michael Berman, National Commander of the Jewish War Veterans, testified in favor of protecting veteran's rights, general health care services, long-term health care, medical research, construction of new medical facilities, improved funding for Post Traumatic Stress Disorder (PTSD), priority care for veterans who received the Purple Heart Award, and preservation of national cemeteries.[63]

The Jewish War Veterans (JWV), Michael Berman, its legislative director stated that the group had fought for the right to fair and appropriate compensation for its veterans for over 100 years. He noted that there were more than 25 million veterans in the United States, and over seven million of them were over 64 years of age. He expressed the sentiment of the organization by pointing out how Congress consistently limited veteran's benefits. Berman asserted that any additional reduction of veteran's benefits were unreasonable and would be viewed as a disservice to veterans who faithfully served the United States.[64]

Furthermore, the JWV stated that the Balanced Budget Act was having an adverse effect on the funding of health care programs for veterans. For example, Berman cited that budget cuts diminished available hospital services for veterans, pensions, and prescription drugs. He emphatically lamented the fact that veterans were being treated like second-class citizens. Consequently, the Jewish War Veterans strongly opposed any changes to veteran's legislation that would result in reductions of their benefits. While vigorously urging Congress to pass a budget that would fully fund and preserve the integrity of all the veteran's entitlement programs.[65]

Berman urged Congress to support increased funding for medical research on veteran's issues. The organization also proposed that legislation be passed that would increase the number of outpatient services available to veterans in need of specialized care. The Jewish War Veterans (JWV) encouraged Congress to provide adequate funding for new VA construction and program modernization or replacement of old, obsolete facilities. It supported the creation of a system that would determine construction priorities on whether it would ensure the improved quality of veteran's health care in the end. In addition, the organization suggested that VA hospitals be reconfigured to create new long-term care facilities for aging veterans with emphasis placed on areas with higher percentages of "empty beds" in nursing facilities. The organization also argued in favor of funding for Post-Traumatic Stress Disorder so that veterans suffering with PTSD and substance abuse could receive counseling in clean and safe treatment facilities. Congress should increase national oversight of the program. In addition, no inpatient programs should be closed unless there were adequate support services are available in the community.[66]

Apart from the above, Berman expressed the organization's opposition to the attempts made by the federal government relinquish responsibility for National Cemeteries to the states. The cemeteries, he submitted, should not only remain in federal hands but should also be better funded and staffed. Finally, he argued in support of placing recipients of the Purple Heart Award in a priority category that would qualify them for medical services at facilities operated by the Veteran's Administration (VA).[67]

In addition to the testimony of Michael Berman for the Jewish War Veterans (JWV), Roger Putnam of the Non-Commissioned Officers Association (NCOA) also testified before the Joint Veteran's Affairs Committees on March 4, 1999. His testimony stressed the following points: (1) provide affordable and equitable medical benefits for veterans and their families; (2) enhance the Montgomery GI Bill; (3) revise the employment program; (4) collaborate with the Budget and Armed Services Committees to develop a funding plan for veteran's entitlement programs; and (5) establish an "aggressive" timeline to implement programmatic changes.[68]

The Non-Commissioned Officers Association (NCOA) further urged Congress to provide improved comprehensive health care and medical treatment for veterans. The group noted in its testimony on February 11, 1999 that the 2000 Budget proposal for the Department of Veteran's Affairs failed to adjust for the cost of inflation. The organization alleged that the budget proposal also exaggerated cost savings and the impact of third party collections for VA health care services. Putnam charged the Veteran's Administration (VA) with providing decreased services to veterans due to inadequate funding.[69] While the NCOA acknowledged that the VA had cut costs by utilizing outpatient facilities and services when appropriate, the group suggested that Medicare subvention would further reduce the cost of implementing the health care component of veteran's benefits. In addition, the group asserted that the VA is extremely dependent on outside funding for health care services. Consequently, the NCOA suggested that Medicare subvention would save money over the long-term while providing improved health care for Department of Veteran's Affairs and the Department of Defense.[70]

The Non-Commissioned Officers Association (NCOA) also expressed its views on the implementation of the "GI Bill." Putnam, on behalf of the group argued in favor of educational reforms. While the organization was pleased with program enhancements made in 1998 and the 20% increase in the entitlement program, it stressed that the education benefits remain inadequate. It also called attention to the fact that the Veteran's Transition Commission listed the education benefit program as one that needed to be reformed. Putnam stated that less than 40% of program participants utilized the education benefit, despite the fact that 96% of all recruits enrolled in the program. The overwhelming majority (56%) of veterans enrolled in the education benefit program failed to participate in the program because the increase in the entitlement appropriations simply was not enough to cover tuition costs at a four-year college. Putnam also pointed to the fact that the "GI Bill" benefit had only increased by 40% since 1985. Thus, the Non-Commissioned Officers Association (NCOA) strongly urged Congress to expand the program and increase its funding in order that more veterans who were enrolled would be able to participate.[71]

Moreover, the NCOA requested that Congress should grant military retirees a higher priority in the VA health care system. The group advised that the Veteran's Administration should be required to provide extended or long-term health care services to military retirees without personal cost to the individuals. The organization maintained that forcing military retirees to pay deductibles and co-payments was unethical and immoral because the majority of the retired veterans gave 20 or more years of "honorable, faithful, and obedient military service."[72] Again, Putnam emphasized the Transition Commission's finding that the departmental policy and law "disenfranchised" military retired veterans in the VA health care system.

Another matter that Putnam addressed was eligibility requirements for burial in Arlington National Cemetery. He urged Congress to enact "meaningful, concise legislation" that would remove special treatment for non-veterans within the memorial affairs division of the veteran's administration. The Non-Commissioned Officers Association (NCOA) argued that the VA should not grant burial space to civilians in veteran's cemeteries because that practice resulted in a lack of burial space for millions of American veterans who, unlike the civilians had fought battles to protect the interest of the United States.[73] The organization argued that since the opportunity to expand Arlington National Cemetery was extremely limited and the four scheduled national cemeteries would not adequately meet even the needs of those World War II veterans, Congress must remedy the situation quickly.[74]

In addition, the NCOA argued that despite the passage of the Veteran's Employment Opportunity Act of 1998, veteran's employment, and training programs continued to be plagued with problems. Putnam insisted that staff at the Department of Veteran's Affairs National Veteran' straining Institute needed to allot additional time to case management, more opportunities for outreach to employers, and the facilitation of transition workshops to assist veterans in experiencing a smooth transition into the workforce following military service.[75] Finally, Putnam expressed the Non-

Commissioned Officers Association's (NCOA) disappointment with the President's fiscal year 2000 budget proposal.[76]

On May 19, 1999, Harley Thomas, legislative director of the Paralyzed Veterans of America, noted the organizations strong support for the language of the "Veteran's Millennium. Health Care Act." The organization's support came about primarily because the legislation was geared towards expanding national long-term care services within facilities operated by the Veteran's Administration. The group also supported the inclusion of provisions directed towards remedying the "reality of exactly which veterans are eligible for nursing-home care and long-term care services".[77] Apart from the foregoing, Thomas also expressed his organization's satisfaction with the bill's goal to provide increased assistance to veterans who required specialized care such as veterans suffering with spinal cord dysfunction (SCD). Since veterans with specialized needs such as SCD relied heavily on the availability of long-term care beds that were constructed and manufactured specifically for the VA. The legislation, he continued, should "clearly acknowledge access to special patient populations" such as veterans who are paralyzed and suffering with spinal cord dysfunction.[78]

While the Paralyzed Veterans of America (PVA) supported the general merits of the bill, the group voiced serious concerns about the provision allowing increases in co-payments charged to veterans for health care services given by the Veterans Health Administration under the auspices of the Department of Veteran's Affairs. In fact, Thomas, testifying before the Veteran Subcommittee on Health and Hospitals, argued that if the co-payment provision, which authorized the Department of Veteran's Affairs to revise the co-payment requirement for services, remained in the proposed legislation, such an increase in co-payments would result in a retrenchment of previous eligibility requirements. In addition, the organization noted its concern that the Veteran's Administration (VA) had serious difficulties collecting fees under the previous co-payment plan. It therefore, expressed doubts whether the VA would be able to collect more successfully under the new plan or be able to formulate and implement a co-payment schedule that could be uniformly applied to all veterans. As a result, the Paralyzed Veterans of America (PVA) concluded that while the goal of H.R. 2116 -- The Veteran's Millennium Health Care Act (VMHCA) was well intentioned; it held little faith that the Department of Veteran's Affairs would develop a plan that would be fair and equitable for veterans.[79]

The legislative assistant for The Retired Enlisted Association (TREA), John Daly, in his testimony before the House Veteran's Affairs Subcommittee on Health, argued in favor of the creation of a specific category for military retirees, who had previously lost access to medical facilities administered by the Department of Veteran's Affairs and the Veteran's Health Administration. The provision that he was suggesting would correct the above oversight and thereby benefit individuals/retirees who had served twenty or more years in the United States Armed Services.[80]

Furthermore, The Retired Enlisted Association (TREA) argued the military retirees often had few options for medical and health care services. The group noted that TRICARE, the Department of Defense's (DOD) health care program on which most military retirees depended was not well administered by DOD. Physicians were opting out of the program because of low reimbursement rates and delays in processing medical claims. Many retirees, like many veterans, witnessed the closing of a number of military treatment facilities in their geographic areas. As a consequence, many retirees lost access to the TRICARE program network. The Association approved the provisions in the bill that were specifically aimed at improving long-term care for veterans as well as increasing veterans access to health care services. John Daly concluded that the "Veteran's Millennium Health Care Act (VMHCA)" represented the federal government's praiseworthy effort at providing "guaranteed" benefits to retirees of the United States Armed Forces.[81]

On May 19, 1999, Vietnam Veterans of America's (VVA) Director of Government Relations, Richard Weidman shared his views on the legislative proposal. He argued that shortages in resources were widespread and that they were having a profound effect on the implementation of veteran's health care and benefit programs. He continued, Congress must increase the funds it was providing the Department of Veteran's Affairs so that it could administer the entitlement programs more effectively. Failure to do so would lead to the destruction of the Veteran's Health Administration, which would in turn, adversely affect American veterans.[82]

The Vietnam Veterans of America (VVA) favored the provision in the bill prohibiting the Department of Veteran's Affairs from reducing the number of beds or available space in its nursing facilities. Furthermore, Weidman maintained that the VA's capacity to assist veterans in need of mental health services (i.e., Post -Traumatic

Stress Disorder, substance abuse, sexual harassment) had been decimated by remedial efforts to restructure its mental health component. The Veteran's Administration focused much of its attention on rebuilding in areas that heavily dealt with veterans who needed "specialized services" (such as Spinal Cord Injury, and Post Traumatic Stress Disorder.[83]

The organization supported a "reasonable" co-payment requirement for medical devices and prescription drugs for those veterans with the financial resources to pay. It also favored the section of the bill dealing with co-payments for medical treatment unrelated to a veteran's military service. It complained gravely that many veterans were billed for prescription drugs and devices, which were related conditions sustained while serving in the military. Thus, the organization recommended that if the department was going to continue billing veterans for prescription drugs and medical devices such as hearing aids, the co-payment requirements should be implemented with increased sensitivity.[84]

The VVA also agreed with the provision in the proposed legislation that extended priority care status to former prisoners of war and recipients of the "Purple Heart Award" regardless of "service connected" disability status or income level. This really showed the truism in the Veteran's health care Administration's motto: "Caring for he (or she) who hath Borne the Battle."[85]

Apart from the above, Richard Weidman, Director of Government Relations of the organization argued in favor of the following for increased reporting requirements and the strengthening of the adult day care and respite care services, that the Secretary of the Department of Veteran's Affairs should be required to provide long-term services as a veteran entitlement, and the proposal to create a "Veteran's Tobacco Trust Fund." Such a fund, he asserted would enhance the ability of the Department not only to implement an improved and user-friendly smoking cessation program but also to do the same for veterans. [86] Having stated the above, he then proceeded to deal with the Balanced Budget Act which his organization considered to be full of inequities against veterans. Furthermore, he noted that if the fiscal year 2000 and 2001 budgetary appropriations remained inadequate, the already overly stressed and "brittle system" would continue to erode. Thus, the Vietnam Veterans of America maintained that unless budget appropriations were greatly increased, "veterans will literally die from neglect."[87]

The organizations of veterans utilized the media to inform and sensitize the public to their concerns about the state of veteran's health care and benefit programs in the United States. A number of news stories were ran on long-term health care inpatient and outpatient services, the Department of Veteran's Affairs budget and the impact of inadequate appropriations in the various media. For example, the media covered stories in which individual veterans and veterans groups sought judicial redress for their concerns. This approach was used as a last resort in their line of efforts designed to plead their case for improved "lifetime" health care services and benefits.[88]

In July of 1999, one month following the introduction of the Veteran's Millennium Health Care Act (VMHCA) - H.R. 2116, the *Orange County Register* reported on the Veteran's Millennium Health Care Act (VMHCA) and the goal of the bill. The news article described the bill as an attempt by Congress to shift veteran's health care services from a system based on large centralized hospitals to a system focussing primarily on outpatient clinics, community-based health care and facilities and long-term health care services.[89]

The Washington Post reported a story on the manner in which the federal government funded veteran's health care and the impact of the Balanced Budget Act of 1997 on veteran health care. The article emphasized that funding for veteran's health care had been essentially frozen since the passage of the Balanced Budget Act of 1997. Consequently, health care costs outpaced the financial resources of the Department of Veteran's Affairs. During this same period, the demand for care services administered by the department surpassed the availability of the VA health care. Because of the freeze on funding and the increased demand for medical services, the condition of the Veteran's Administration's health care system was exacerbated by the increasing aging population of veterans and the systematic abandonment of numerous veterans and military retirees. Both veterans and military retirees experienced decreased access due to military base closures in the mid to late 1980s.[90]

In an effort to further prompt Congress into action, veteran's interest groups pointed to a Government Accounting Office (GAO) report on costs associated with the implementation of veteran's entitlement programs. They stressed that GAO estimated that the VA wasted close to $1 million a day on maintaining old, unused, or inefficient buildings. Furthermore, the groups noted that GAO spent approximately $35 million a year to maintain 5 million square feet of vacant space owned by the Department of Veteran's Affairs. Therefore, veteran's pressure groups surmised that due to poor asset management, the Veteran's Administration (VA) spent close to 25 percent of its budget operating and maintaining roughly 4,700 facilities and 18,000 acres of land in 181 sites.[91] As such, veteran's pressure groups maintained the funds should have otherwise been spent on programs that would have increased veteran's access to medical care.

The paper urged both the House and Senate to adequately fund health care for veterans and military retirees who "have borne the battle" in defense of the United States and its interests abroad. Therefore, it was suggested that Congress should adopt the provisions of the American Legion's "GI Bill of Health," which that organization's representative had submitted at the hearings. The plan could reduce the health care systems' dependence on tax dollars by utilizing third party funding, and at the same time allowing the VA to service more veterans especially military retirees and elderly veterans.[92]

In short, veteran's organizations supported the legislation with virtually little dissent. This was due largely to the fact that the legislation was aimed at improving and enhancing veteran's health care services and benefits. Many of the provisions included in the bill either were taken directly or indirectly from the testimony of veteran's organizations, state agencies responsible for administering services to veterans or the executive branch's admission of policy and programmatic deficiencies. The Act was embraced because under the previous law, the VA provided America's veterans with long-term care services through placing them in nursing home facilities. However, many veterans who were eligible for such nursing care services failed to receive care due to a lack of available space. Thus, many veterans throughout the country were forced to go without the long-term care or nursing care services they needed simply because the Veteran's Administration was unable to secure adequate space. Therefore, House bill H.R. 2116 mandated that the Veteran's Administration (VA) must provide such services through alternative programs such as home care services and adult day care facilities. Prior to H.R. 2116, veterans in dire need of long-term health care services were placed in VA or state operated nursing home facilities or waitlisted for spaces in such facilities.[93]

The *U.S. Newswire* reported a story in which the organization maintained that the action of the government "is immoral" and aimed at making the claims process more difficult for veterans. It also claimed that the VA failed to comply with its own regulations that required the department to notify the public or publicly comment on major policy shifts.[94]

Veterans Seek Redress Through Litigation

After years of lobbying and pleading for improved veteran's health care services and benefits, a number of veterans and veteran's organizations saw the judicial system as the last avenue for redress of their complaints. For example, the Coalition of Retired Military Veterans filed a claim against the Department of Justice government in an effort to force the government to restore "lifetime health care benefits" to military retirees. The organization claimed that veterans were promised "lifetime" health care when they enlisted in the military. Specifically, the Coalition stated that, "We're not freeloaders. We just want what we were told we had when we signed up." The group, which consisted of 9,000 members, filed a lawsuit with the U.S. Circuit Court of Appeals, asking that judicial body to compel the government to fulfill "its promise." The Coalition of Retired Military Veterans maintained that the government promised "lifetime" health care as a benefit of service in the military, but that it had managed to successfully defraud approximately 2,5000,000 military retirees. The organization lost. Its attorney, Michael Kator, having noted the group's disappointment with the dismissal of its case, intimated that the organization would consider the following possibilities in its pursuit for "justice": (1) asking the Court of Appeals to reconsider; (2) taking the case to the U.S. Supreme Court; or (3) resubmitting the claim saying that the government had an "implied contract" with the veterans.[95]

The Coalition decided to appeal its case to the Veteran's Court of Appeals. This body ruled that the U.S. Justice Department had not violated any regulation. In fact, the court, in its ruling clearly stated that it had found no military regulation that called for the provision of "unconditional lifetime" free medical care. Recruiters' promises of free health care services, according to the court were only an "inducement". Congress should resolve the issue of providing medical care to military retirees and the President perorated the court.[96]

Another veteran's organization, Class Action Group (CAG) sued the federal government for "lifetime" health care services. The group originally filed suit against the Department of Veteran's Affairs in 1995 when U.S. military hospitals and medical facilities began turning away career personnel due to budget cuts and military base closures. The content of the suit was virtually identical to the argument made in the earlier suit filed by the Coalition of Retired Military Veterans against the Justice Department. The CAG suit was dismissed on similar grounds as the previous case argued by the Coalition of Retired Military Veterans.[97]

Despite this loss, CAG continued to press the argument that the government promised "lifetime medical services" and that military retirees and veterans earned, "free medical care for life." The group, headed by an attorney, George (Bud) Day, a retired Air Force Colonel and Medal of Honor recipient, a former prisoner of war and cellmate of Senator John McCain's in North Vietnam filed suit in a federal court in Pensacola, Florida on behalf of those men and women (65 or older) who joined the military prior to June 1956, when the Department of Defense health care system was reorganized. The group demanded that the Pentagon be mandated to provide free medical care and that "Part B" Medicare premiums paid by retirees be refunded.[98]

In 1998, U.S. District Court Judge Roger Vinson found that the organization had a "strong equitable argument" in favor of the government abiding by its promise to America's veterans and military retirees. However, he concluded that ruling in favor of the CAG would tantamount to a violation of the separation of powers clause in the Constitution.[99] Day appealed the decision to the U.S. Court of Appeals. During the appeal, lawyers for the Department of Defense acknowledged that recruiters had made promises of "free medical care" for life because they were instructed to do so by top military officials in Washington, D.C. They further argued that the promises were made but were not legally binding. The suit is pending in the courts. It is important to note that this case is still pending before the U.S. Court of Appeals. Therefore, the judicial ruling is not available.[100]

In a suit that was dismissed the Veteran's Affairs Legislative Court, Navy retiree Donald L. Moore, like many veterans, assumed that free health care would be provided in return for his military service. The assumption was in fact valid because for decades, the military provided health care services to him while he worked as a civilian following his retirement. Physicians at VA administered facilities treated Moore, his wife and three children. He "never" received a bill for any of the medical treatment he and his family received. He believed the government was returning benefits to him for his years of military service until he received a bill for medical treatment previously provided to him and his family. In his suit, Moore argued that he and his family received "free" medical treatment for years and never received a medical bill from the Veteran's Administration, he justifiably believed that free medical care to veterans should be continued. Moore emphasized his disillusionment; he felt "abandoned by the nation" he so diligently and proudly served.[101] Moore's suit for reinstatement of the previous policy of provided free medical services was unsuccessful. The legislative court which heard his appeal found the suit to be without merit and therefore, dismissed by the legislative court.

Another case, (*Morton v. West* [12 Vet. App. 477]) was filed by a veteran who argued that the department's newly revised policy of no longer assisting veterans develop their initial claims for disability compensation was illegal. The plaintiff, Jack Morton, a veteran first submitted claims for hearing loss, varicose veins, a back disorder and a shortening or lengthening of the right upper portion of his body to the Department of Veteran's Affairs and the Board of Veteran's Appeals (BVA). Both entities determined that the claims were unsubstantiated as service-connected injuries. Morton argued that the VA's administrative regulations Manual M21-1 on the development of VA claims, stipulated that the Veteran's Administration (VA) would provide assistance to veterans attempting to develop a "well-grounded" claim, while veterans continued to be treated by VA physicians. However, the Board of Veteran's Affairs (BVA) was not required to assist veterans in fully developing their medical claims. To make matters worse, the U.S. Court of Appeals for Veteran's Claims and for the Federal Circuit both held that 38 U.S.C. Section 5107(a) stipulated that if a veteran failed to submit a "well-grounded claim the veteran is not entitled to VA medical benefits."[102] The implications of the case could very well have an enormous impact on the manner in which the Department of Veteran's Affairs assists veterans develop their medical claims. More importantly, the ruling would have a profound effect on the number of veterans who would be able to document their injury or illness as being related to their service in the armed services. Therefore, the number of veterans who would be eligible for VA health care services would sharply decrease due to their inability to prove that their illness or injuries were directly related to their years of military service.

The change in departmental policy required that regional staff should withhold assistance to veterans until the Veteran's Administration (VA) determined claims to be "well grounded." It is crucial to note that this reversal of a long-standing departmental policy to assist veterans who filed claims for compensation has adversely affected the number of claims that are successfully filed. This continues to be a frustrating experience for disabled veterans.[103]

Ronald Flagg, American Legion's attorney, maintained that the policy change created a "Catch 22" because the previous standard "always held the veteran was entitled to benefits if the claim was well-grounded."[104] He submitted that veterans could not formulate a well-grounded claim without the assistance of the Veteran's Administration. Indeed, he argued that if the VA did not provide veterans with help in filing medical claims, veterans would be unable to present a "well-grounded" claim. The American Legion asserted its belief that the department changed the policy with full knowledge of the fact that the majority of veterans needed assistance in obtaining the documentation that linked their current health condition to their military service. The American Legion concluded that the VA decision to change the policy was aimed at reducing the number of claims the department would have to approve. He added that veterans must prove that their claims were "well-grounded" prior to the claim being administered by the Veteran's Administration.[105] In addition, the attorney for the American Legion noted that "if the veteran already had documentation in hand to submit a well-grounded claim" then he or she would not need assistance from the Veteran's Administration.[106] He suggested that the cost of new self-paid medical examinations alone -- which are necessary to prove a veteran's claim -- would impact tens of thousands of veterans because they lacked the financial resources to pay co-payments for their doctor's visits in an attempt to file a "well-grounded" claim for medical assistance under the current policy of the Department of Veteran's Affairs. The organization estimated that the medical examinations alone would cost veterans "tens of millions of dollars a year." In fact, if veterans had access to funds to finance medical treatment provided by private physicians, it was likely that they would opt out of the VA health care system.[107]

As a result of the shift in the VA's policy, the American Legion filed suit against the Department of Veteran's Affairs on the grounds that no government agency may "unilaterally repeal regulations" dealing with the rights of individuals by merely "declaring that the earlier regulations were just a mistake."[108] The Court of Veteran's Appeals found in favor of the government. The veteran's group declared that the Court of Appeals ruling was a case of "judicial overreaching," and placed a restriction on the Secretary of the Department of Veteran's Affairs that does not exist."[109] The court ruled in *Morton v. West* that Secretary of the Department of Veteran's Affairs Togo West was not obligated to assist veterans in filing a "well-grounded" claim for medical treatment in the VA system.

Following the ruling in the *Morton v. West* case the American Legion received a letter from the Department of Veteran's Affairs, which indicated that despite the fact that veterans were previously treated in military hospitals, the VA did not assume the responsibility for obtaining records "unless the claimant has submitted a well-grounded claim." However, the Department of Veteran's Affairs spokesperson, Ken McKinnon assured veterans organizations that the VA "will continue in some fashion to help veterans develop their claim" despite the court's ruling.[110] Consequently, it is unclear as to the number of veterans who filed claims and who may have been adversely affected by the change in departmental policy, the Court of Appeals (for Veteran's Claims) ruling, and the discretion exercised by VA regional staff to decide whether to assist a veteran in filing a claim or place the entire burden of proving a medical claim on the veteran.[111]

Interest groups utilized various strategies and tactics, i.e., face-to face meetings, letter-writing and telephone campaigns, etc., to convey their policy preferences. Additionally, they used the Internet to facilitate communication between organizations, members, and the public. Through use of the "World-Wide Web," they kept their constituency or members informed of legislative actions taken on House bill H. R. 2116. Each group utilized this medium to communicate its political agenda with veterans. Veteran's organizations maintained websites with links to their newspapers and magazines. The Veteran's Millennium Health Care Act of (VMHCA) was reported in veteran's newspapers and magazines. This approach allowed those interested in veteran's issues to access information on the VMHCA at their convenience. Consequently, the advent of the "World-Wide Web" affords interest groups an opportunity unlike any other - to communicate with millions of people with the click of a button.

Testimony of State Veteran's Homes Administrators

The President of the National Association of State Veteran's Homes (NASVH), Robert Shaw in his testimony before the Subcommittee on Health echoed ideas on issues such as long-term health care, payments to state veteran's homes, and construction grants for state operated nursing home facilities. Shaw noted that the objective of construction grants for state home facilities was to assist states in either purchasing or building nursing home facilities that will satisfy nursing care needs of veterans residing in state administered facilities. In instances when state agencies purchase a facility, VA construction or renovation grants only covered for 65 percent of the estimate for constructing new buildings and purchasing the initial equipment. [112] The remaining necessary funds must be acquired by state agencies without federal assistance. Generally, state legislatures bore the responsibility for providing them in to complete the construction or renovation project.[113]

Since the inception of the grant program, subsequent legislation has made many changes in it as well as giving it permanent status. The Department of Veteran's Affairs fiscal year 2000 Budget indicated that one hundred forty-one (141) new projects were added to the existing ones, thereby increasing the number of spaces in state operated nursing home facilities by 20,139. In addition, the department remarked that there were approximately 180 State nursing home facilities needed to be remodeled or renovated in order to meet fire safety regulations.[114]

The organization (NASVH) noted that the method by which construction grants were awarded showed a preference for construction projects that were geared towards increasing the availability of beds in nursing facilities. In general, new facilities were given priority over renovated buildings. The criteria used in VA construction grants placed requests to construct a new facility at the top because creating new buildings was considered the easiest way to ensure an increase in the available number of beds or space available. On the other hand, renovation projects only ensured that the available number of beds would not decrease. Consequently, the National Association for State Veteran's Homes offered a suggestion that future grant proposals or requests should be prioritized in the year they were received, following current Department of Veteran's Affairs needs criteria. However, future project proposals should not be funded until projects submitted in previous years were funded. This meant, of course, that all grants received in 2000 would be reviewed and ranked. Grant proposals submitted by organizations that were out of funding range would be given priority over applications for the year 2001. Ultimately, Robert Shaw, president of the organization, argued the above recommendation would ensure that every nursing facility was maintained because new projects could be built while maintaining the viability of state homes. Shaw gallantly suggested that proposals from States that lacked a State nursing home facility should automatically become eligible for funding for its first facility irrespective of the year the grant proposal was submitted. He maintained that the primary reason that State officials had been unwilling to appropriate state matching funds for remodeling or renovation projects was due to the fact that the state legislature was unsure that federal matching funds would be available. The organization declared that the adoption of its proposal or strategy would enable States to better plan and anticipate funding time frames. He noted that the organization's scheme would help officials operating state nursing homes to determine when their project would be funded based on the submission date.[115]

Shaw observed that the state veteran's home program had grown from 11 homes in 11 states in 1988 to 95 homes in 43 states in 1999. These facilities provided over 24,000 beds. In fiscal year 1998, state homes provided more than 6.7 million days of nursing home, domiciliary care, and hospital care. Five million three hundred thousand and thirteen veterans received nursing home care. Domiciliary care was provided to 1,323,051 veterans. Finally, 85,030 veterans received hospital care.[116]

The National Association of State Veteran's Homes concluded that the state veterans home care system should be further expanded. The organization contended that the role of state operated veterans homes remained a valuable asset to the Department of Veteran's Affairs because the assistance that it gave had made it possible for states to build more veteran's homes and to introduce innovative steps in providing services to meet a broad range of veteran's needs. As such, the association beckoned on Congress to include the following in the legislation: (1) increased payments to State Veteran's Homes; (2) appropriation of sufficient federal funds to fully fund the backlog of approved grant applications to the VA State Home Construction Grant Program; and (3) modify the method of awarding construction grants by incorporating elements of "first-come, first-served" with the VA's current "needs formula".[117]

Testimony of Health Care Organizations

On April 22, 1999, Steve Watson, administrator of the Ocala Harborside Healthcare Nursing Home and a military retiree, testified on behalf of the American Health Care Association.[118] He expressed the group's (AHCA) concern about long-term care services and the needs of veterans in Ocala, Florida. He asserted that the aging population of veterans required long-term care strategy that would provide the necessary care needed to sustain appropriate health care for these veterans. It was against this backdrop that the association called on the Veteran's Administration (VA) to retain its core VA administered long-term health care services and to continue improving the efficiency of its program operations. Watson remarked that the Administration should continue to meet the demand for increased access to long-term care through existing state veteran's homes and giving contracts to veteran's health care providers. He mentioned that contracting with State veteran's homes gave the Veteran's Administration (VA) the much-needed flexibility necessary to satisfy the increasing demands for medical services. Contracting with state veteran's homes allowed administrators to meet the demand for long-term care services without requiring heavy investment in the development of additional infrastructure. However, Watson stated that the VA did not need to expend departmental funds on expensive construction projects to build new veteran's homes when the funds could be better used to finance medical treatment and services. Therefore, the Association suggested that the VA should commit adequate funding for services to veterans by increasing available beds in nursing homes.[119]

Finally, the AHCA urged Congress and the Department of Veteran's Affairs to continue in its efforts to improve veteran's health care and benefits programs. The organization strongly supported the use of quality indicators and resident satisfaction measurements to monitor and improve the quality of long-term care. Watson also noted that the Veteran's Administration was at the forefront of long-term care in general. He maintained that due to the nature of veteran's health, the VA remained one of the foremost authorities in geriatric treatment for people suffering from chronic illnesses. However, he continued, it was important to note that the association's view of the VA's provision of medical services for veterans differed from those of veteran's organizations such as the Paralyzed Veteran's of America, The Retired Enlisted Association, and the American Legion.[120]

Conclusion

During the first session of the 106th Congress, veteran's organizations like the Paralyzed Veterans of America (PVA), the American Legion, Veterans of Foreign Wars (VFW), Jewish War Veterans (JWV), and the Non-Commissioned Officers Association (NCOA) discussed veteran's health care and benefit issues with members of the House and Senate Joint Veteran's Affairs Committee. Veteran's organization lobbied members of Congress, particularly Senators Arlen Specter (R-PA), Pete Domenici (R-NM), John Rockefeller (D-WV), Representatives Cliff Stearns (R-FL) and Bob Stump (R-AZ). It is crucial to note that much of the information and recommendations made by veteran's organizations were incorporated or utilized in some fashion to shape the original and final version of H.R. 2116 -- the Veteran's Millennium Health Care Act (VMHCA).

The majority of interest groups, i.e. veteran's, state veteran's homes, managed health care, etc., exerted pressure on Congress for veteran's legislation aimed towards redressing problems associated with the delivery of veteran's benefits, particularly medical care services. Accordingly, these interest groups played a vital role in the formulation and passage of the Veteran's Millennium Health Care Act (VMHCA) of 1999. Although initially a Republican bill, it not only was substantially modified, but it particularly included language drafted by Democratic legislators like Minority Leader Senator Tom Daschle and Representative Lane Evans. In fact, shortly after its introduction, House bill H.R. 2116 developed into a bi-partisan bill.

In addition, veteran's groups disseminated information to their members making them aware of the provisions and status of the proposed legislation. These grassroots activities played a fundamental role in the passage of the comprehensive veteran's health care bill. These groups furnished Congress with necessary and cogent information for effective oversight of veteran's entitlement programs. Thus, veteran's organizations were vigilant in their effort to influence the political process in an effort to effect change in the administration of veteran's health care in the United States. Moreover, individual veterans and veteran's organizations legally challenged the Department of Veteran's Affairs and the Department of Justice in federal and legislative courts. Despite their lack of success, in their litigations, they maintained that they would continue to the courts as a means of prompting change in the existing veteran's health care system.

Overall, the participants favored expanding health care benefits and increasing veteran's access to VA medical facilities. Among the group that favored expanding the veteran's health care delivery system were The Retired Enlisted Association (TREA), Non-Commissioned Officers Association (NCOA), Paralyzed Veterans of American (PVA), and the American Legion. However, these organizations opposed increasing copayments or fees charged to veterans for VA medical treatment. Because public opinion polls were not conducted on the veteran's reform legislation, it is impossible to determine how the public's attitude towards veterans affected the formulation and passage of the bill. However, one can surmise that support for veterans has been consistent. This is evident in the extensive history of veteran's entitlement programs. Furthermore, veteran's groups have not faced opposition from other interests. Ultimately, the lack of opposing interest groups ensured the passage of the Veteran's Millennium Health Care Act (VMHCA) by Congress and it's signing by President Clinton.

Notes

---

[1] The Disabled Veteran's Rehabilitation Act, Statutes at Large, 43, 607 (1949).

[2] Gallup Poll [Public Opinion on-line] (Storrs, Conneticut: University of Conneticut 1947-, accessed 30 October 2000); available from the Roper Center, Storrs, Conneticut, accession no. 0206707, p. 1 of 2.

[3] Gallup Poll [Public Opinion on-line] (Storrs, Connecticut: University of Connecticut 1947-, accessed 30 October 2000); available from the Roper Center, Storrs, Connecticut, accession no. 02060708, p. 1 of 2.

[4] Harris and Associates [Public Opinion on-line] (Storrs, Conneticut: University of Conneticut 1953 -, accessed 10 September 2001); available from Roper Center, Storrs, Conneticut, accession no. 0033860, p. 1 of 2.

[5] Harris and Associates [Public Opinion on-line] (Storrs, Conneticut: University of Conneticut 1980 -, accessed 10 September 2001); available from Roper Center, Storrs, Conneticut, accession no. 0355569, p. 1 of 2.

[6] Harris and Associates [Public Opinion on-line] (Storrs, Conneticut: University of Conneticut 1980 -, accessed 10 September 2001); available from Roper Center, Storrs, Conneticut, accession 0355561, p. 1 of 2.

[7] Harris and Associates [Public Opinion on-line] (Storrs, Conneticut: University of Conneticut 1980 -, accessed 10 September 2001); available from Roper Center, Storrs, Conneticut, accession no. 0355562, p. 1 of 2.

[8] Harris and Associates [Public Opinion on-line] (Storrs, Conneticut: University of Conneticut 1980 -, accessed 10 September 2001); available from Roper Center, Storrs, Conneticut, accession no. 0355565, p. 1 of 2.

[9] Harris and Associates [Public Opinion on-line] (Storrs, Conneticut: University of Conneticut 1980 -, accessed 10 September 2001); available from Roper Center, Storrs, Conneticut, accession no. 0004605, p. 1 of 2.

[10] Gallup Poll [Public Opinion on-line] (Storrs, Conneticut: University of Conneticut 1947 -, accessed 30 October 2000); available from Roper Center, Storrs, Conneticut, accession no. 0206708, p. 1 of 2.

[11] Gallup Poll [Public Opinion on-line] (Storrs, Conneticut: University of Conneticut 1984 -, accessed 30 October 2000); available from Roper Center, Storrs, Conneticut, accession no. 0054382, p. 1 of 2.

[12] Harris and Associates [Public Opinion on-line] (Storrs, Conneticut: University of Conneticut 1985 -, accessed 30 October 2000); available from Roper, Storrs, Conneticut, accession no. 0059750, p. 1 of 2.

[13] Gallup Poll [Public Opinion on-line] (Storrs, Conneticut: University of Conneticut 1991 -, accessed 20 October 2000); available from Roper Center, Storrs, Conneticut, accession no. 0043974, p. 1 of 2.

[14] Harris and Associates [Public Opinion on-line] (Storrs, Conneticut: University of Connecticut 1990-, accessed 20 October 2001); available from the Roper Center, Storrs, Conneticut, accession no. 0141061, p. 1 of 2.

[15] Harris and Associates [Public Opinion on-line] (Storrs, Conneticut: University of Connecticut 1991 -, accessed 20 October 2001); available from the Roper Center, Storrs, Conneticut, accession no. 016812, p. 1 of 2.

[16] Harris and Associates [Public Opinion on-line] (Storrs, Conneticut: University of Connecticut 1995-, accessed 30 October 2001); available from

the Roper Center, Storrs, Conneticut, accession no. 0241760, p. 1 of 2. The survey included 1076 adults and an oversample of 307 individuals 65 and over. The senior citizens were weighted to their proportion in the national adult population.

[17] News and Wall Street Journal [Public Opinion on-line] (Storrs, Conneticut: University of Connecticut 1996-, accessed 20 October 2001); available from the Roper Center, Storrs, Conneticut, accession no. 0270074, p. 1 of 3.

[18] Los Angeles Times [Public Opinion on-line] (Storrs, Conneticut: University of Connecticut 1996-, accessed 20 October 2001); available from the Roper Center, Storrs, Conneticut, accession no. 0273013, p. 1 of 3.

[19] Mathew Greenwald Associates [Public Opinion on-line] (Storrs, Conneticut: University of Connecticut 1999-, accessed 20 October 2001); available from the Roper Center, Storrs, Conneticut, accession no. 0331549, p. 1 of 3.

[20]*Federalist* (Hammondsworth: Penguin, 1987), 79.

[21] Jeffrey Berry, *The Interest Group Society* (United States: Harper Collins Publishers, 1977), 3.

[22] Jeffrey Berry, *Lobbying for the People* (New Jersey: Princeton University Press, 1977), 7.

[23] Jeffrey Berry, *Lobbying for the People* (New Jersey: Princeton University Press, 1977).

[24] Ibid., 263.

[25] Abraham Holtzman, *Interest Groups and Lobbying* (New York: Macmillan Company, 1966), 10-11.

[26] Jack Walker, "The Origins and Maintenance of Interest Groups in America," *American Political Science Review*, vol. 77, no. 2 (June 1983), 400-401.

[27] Arthur Bentley, *The Process of Government* (Bloomington: The Principia Press, Inc., 1935).

[28] Ibid.

[29] David Truman, *The Governmental Process* (New York: Alfred A. Knopf, 1951).

[30] Ibid.

[31] Jeffrey Berry, *The Interest Group Society* (New York: Harper Collins Publisher, 1989), 4.

[32] Ibid., 5-6.

[33] Ibid., 5.

[34] Ibid., 6-7.

[35] V. O. Key, *Politics, Parties and Pressure Groups* 3rd ed. (New York: Thomas Cromwell Company, 1953), 25-28.

[36] Ibid., 53-56.

[37] Ibid., 87-89.

[38] Ibid., 119-121.

[39] Ibid.

[40] Hanes Walton, *Black Politics* (Philadelphia: Lippencott, 1972).

[41] Jeffrey Berry, *Lobbying for the People* (New Jersey, Princeton University Press, 1977), 267.

[42] Ibid.

[43] V.O. Key, *Politics, Parties and Interest Groups,* 3rd ed. (New York: Thomas Cromwell Company, 1952), 122.

[44] Ibid.

[45] Ibid.

[46] Justin Gray, *The Inside Story of the Legion* (New York: Boni and Gaer, 1948), 232.

[47] V.O. Key, *Politics, Parties and Pressure Groups* 3rd ed. (New York: Thomas Cromwell Company, 1952), 124.

[48] Ibid.

[49] Ibid., 124-126.

[50] Steve Robertson, "Annual Report to the National Legislative Commission," *American Legion* (November 8, 2000). A copy of the electronic mail response from Mr. Robertson is included in the Appendices. Also included is a copy of the annual report presented to the American Legion's Legislative Commission which briefly discusses P.L. 106-117, formerly House bill H.R. 2116 – the Veteran's Millennium Health Care Act of 1999.

[51] U.S. Congress, House and Senate, Joint Committee on Veteran's Affairs, Subcommittee on Hospitals and Health, *The Impact of Budget Shortfalls on the Delivery of Health Care to Rural Veterans*, 100th Cong., 1st sess., 2 December 1988, 31.

[52] Ibid.

[53] U.S. Congress, House and Senate, Joint Committee on Veteran's Affairs, Subcommittee on Health and Hospitals, The *Proposed Veteran's Millennium Health Care Act*, Report by Thomas A. Pouliot, 106th Cong., 1st sess., 1999, 1-2.

[54] Ibid.

[55] Ibid.

[56] Ibid.

[57] Ibid., 3.

[58] Ibid.

[59] Ibid., 4.

[60] Ibid., 4-5.

[61] Ibid., 5.

[62] Ibid.

[63] U.S. Congress, House and Senate, Joint Committee on Veteran's Affairs, Subcommittee on Health and Hospitals, The *Proposed Veteran's Millennium Health Care Act*, Report by Michael Berman, 106th Cong., 1st sess., 1999, 1-11.

[64] Ibid., 2.

[65] Ibid., 3.

[66] Ibid., 5, 6

[67] Ibid., 8.

[68] U.S. Congress. House and Senate. Joint Committee on Veteran's Affairs. Subcommittee on Health and Hospitals. *The Proposed Veteran's Millennium Health Care Act*. Report by Roger Putnam. 106th Cong., 1st sess., 1999 [database on-line] available from http://www.veterans.house.gov/hearings/schedule106/mar99/3-4-99/ncoa.htm; Internet; accessed 29 April 2000, 4.

[69] Ibid.

[70] Ibid., 7-8.

[71] Ibid., 5.

[72] Ibid.

[73] Ibid., 12.

[74] Ibid., 13.

[75] Ibid., 12.

[76] Ibid., 8.

[77] U.S. Congress, House and Senate, Joint Committee on Veteran's Affairs, Subcommittee on Health and Hospitals, The *Proposed Veteran's Millennium Health Care Act, Report* by Harley Thomas, 106th Cong., 1st sess., 1999 [database on-line] available from

---

http://www.veterans.house.gov/va/hearings/schedule106/5-19-99/pva.htm; Internet; accessed 1 April 2000, 4.

[78] Ibid.

[79] Ibid.

[80] U.S. Congress, House and Senate, Joint Committee on Veteran's Affairs, Subcommittee on Health and Hospitals, The *Proposed Veteran's Millennium Health Care Act,* Report by John Daly, 106th Cong., 1st sess., 1999 [database on-line] available from http://www.house.gov/va/hearings/schedule106/may99/5-19-99/trea.htm; Internet; accessed 1 August 2000, 2.

[81] Ibid.

[82] U.S. Congress, House and Senate, Joint Committee on Veterans Affairs, Subcommittee on Health and Hospital, The *Veteran's Millennium Health Care Act,* Report by Richard Weidman, 106th Cong., 1st sess., 1999 [database on-line] available from http://www.veterans.house.gove/hearings/schedule106/may99/5-19-99/vva.htm; Internet; accessed 1 April 2000, 1.

[83] Ibid., 2.

[84] Ibid., 3.

[85] Ibid.

[86] Ibid., 2-3.

[87] Ibid, 5-6.

[88] Ibid., 6.

[89] Jennifer Maddox, "Changes to Veterans Care sought HEALTH: The House is scheduled to consider a bill that shifts focus to outpatient clinics and long-term and community programs," *Orange County Register* (Santa Ana), 27 July 1999, A5.

[90] Chester Steller, "Keeping the Faith with Veterans," *The Washington Post* (Washington, D.C.), 18 August 1999, A18.

[91] Ibid.

[92] Ibid.

[93] Ibid.

[94] "American Legion Sues Department of Veteran's Affairs," *U.S. Newswire*, 12 October 1999,1.

[95] "Veterans Groups To Sue Again," *The Augusta Chronical* (Augusta), 11 August 1999, C11.

[96] Mark Pratt, "Appeals Court Says Veterans Not Guaranteed Health Care," *The Plain Dealer*, (Cleveland, OH), 11 August 1999, A17.

[97] "Broken Promises," *St. Louis Post-Dispatch*, (St. Louis), 18 August 1999, B6.

[98] Jeff Nesmith, "Veterans Fight For Promise," *Dayton Daily News* (Dayton), 15 March 2000, A1.

[99] Ibid., 2.

[100] Ibid.

[101] Robert Suro and Eric Peann," Battle Cry for Free Health Care; Retired Veterans Push Congress to Restore Promised Benefit." *The Washington Post* (Washington, D.C.), 26 March 2000, A16.

[102] *Morton v. West* [12 Vet.App.477 (1999)].

[103] "American Legion Sues Department of Veteran's Affairs," *U.S. Newswire*, 12 October 1999, 1.

[104] John Hanchette, "Major Change in VA Policy Has American Legion Up in Arms," *Arizona Republic* (Phoenix), 17 October 1999, A14-15.

[105] Ibid.

[106] Ibid.

---

[107] Ibid.

[108] Ibid., A15.

[109] Ibid.

[110] Ibid.

[111] Ibid.

[112] The program for assembling State Home facilities with construction plans began on August 19, 1964 when Public Law 88-450 was enacted and authorized annual appropriations of $5 million dollars for making grants to state operated nursing facilities by the Department of Veteran's Affairs. In 1964, the law limited the amount of the grant to 50 percent of the cost of construction; expansion or remodeling buildings for use as nursing care facilities, and the entitled purchase of equipment.

[113] U.S. Congress. House and Senate. Joint Committee on Veteran's Affairs. Subcommittee on Health and Hospitals. *The Proposed Veteran's Millennium Health Care Act.* Report by Robert Shaw, 106th Cong., 1st sess., 1999.,1.

[114] Ibid., 3.

[115] Ibid.

[116] Ibid., 3.

[117] Ibid., 4-5.

[118] U.S. Congress, House and Senate, Joint Committees on Veteran's Affairs, *The Veteran's Millennium Health Care Act*, 106th Cong., 1st sess., 22 April 1999; 1-4.

[119] Ibid., 1-2.

[120] Ibid., 4.

CHAPTER 5

THE VETERAN'S MILLENNIUM HEALTH CARE ACT

The Veteran's Millennium Health Care Act (VMHCA) - H.R. 2116 was introduced by Representative Cliff Stearns (R-FL) on June 9, 1999. The House of Representatives passed the Veteran's Millennium Health Care Act (VMHCA) on September 21, 1999 by a vote of 369-46. The Senate passed the bill on November 5, 1999 by unanimous consent. House and Senate Conferees worked diligently to produce a conference bill that both chambers could embrace.[1] The Conference Report 106-470 passed the House of Representatives on November 16, 1999 under "suspension of the rules". The bill passed the Senate on November 19, 1999 by unanimous consent. President William Jefferson Clinton signed it on November 30, 1999.

The Act amended Title 38 of the United States Code, which covered veteran's entitlements. The new law mandated that the U.S. Department of Veteran' Affairs improve veteran's access to long-term care for disabled veterans. It enhanced both the health care and educational benefits as well. The legislation addressed the problem of burial space shortages in veteran's cemeteries by providing funds for the establishment of new ones.

This chapter discusses Titles I through XI of P.L. 106-117, the Veteran's Millennium Health Care Act. The new law contains more than seventy (70) major provisions all aimed at enhancing the effectiveness and efficiency of veteran's entitlement programs. Over the last six decades, the VA health care system, which serves veterans in more than 600 locations nationwide, has grown into the nation's largest direct health care provider. During that time, it primarily focused on in-patient care. However, as times changed, it failed to keep pace with societal and medical industry reshapings, which emphasize managed health care. For example, the changing needs of an increasingly aging veteran population continued to strain the VA health care program to such an extent that Congress was forced to insert a special provision in the Act for them.

The VA began to emphasize outpatient care in 1996 when it reformed its system by establishing 22 regional offices. These offices referred to as Veteran's Integrated Service Networks (VISN), were established to make basic budgetary planning and administrative decisions for veterans within specified geographic regions. The VA's goal was to develop local or regional networks of health care providers that offer a continuum of services in ambulatory settings. Title I, Subtitle A of the law addressed long-term care. The law increased veteran's access to medical care by requiring the VA to operate and maintain extended care programs, i.e., respite care, community based nursing home care, and adult day health care. The department was also allowed to develop institutional alternatives to improve the delivery of health care services.

The legislation required the Department of Veteran's Affairs to provide nursing care services for veterans in need of extended care services. Title I, Subtitle A of the bill compelled the department to provide nursing home care to all veterans who suffered from "service-connected" disabilities. In addition, such nursing home care must be provided by the Veteran's Administration (VA) to those veterans suffering from a service-connected disability of at least 70 percent. In an effort to ensure that veterans had a voice in the medical facility in which they receive nursing care, Title I of the Act mandated that the nursing home care facilities must obtain the consent of veterans or their family representatives prior to transferring them to other nursing facilities. In the event that space was unavailable in a VA facility, the department was authorized to contract with community-based facilities in order to comply with the new law and thereby increase veteran's access to nursing home care.[2]

Furthermore, in an attempt to provide increased entree into extended health care services to veterans, H.R. 2116 required that the Department of Veteran's Affairs should administer nursing home care, adult day health care, respite care, home care services (domiciliary), a well as non-institutional alternatives to nursing home care. In addition, P.L. 106-117 removed the six-month limit on the provision of adult day health care. It further required the Department of Veteran's Affairs to furnish respite care services to all eligible veterans. For the first time in the history of the veteran's health care entitlement program, Congress gave the Veteran's Administration the ability to contract out "respite care" services. Prior to the enactment of the new law, in similar situations where the spouse or relative charged with caring for a veteran needed a break from providing home care for a veteran, the caregiver would be forced to wait for available space in a state or VA operated nursing home facility. In addition, the responsibility for transporting the veteran to the available site created another obstacle for family caregivers because veteran's families typically lacked the financial or proper equipment necessary to transport veterans to a new facility. As a result of the 1999 Act, family members were no longer forced to wait for available space in a state-operated nursing home or VA facility. The 1999 law gave some comfort to families by providing medical services to relatives who desired to care for veterans in their home. The law required that family members who cared for veterans were entitled to home-based support services aimed at reducing the burden and stress typically associated with family home-care providers. Moreover, the department was mandated to furnish adult day health care services to veterans enrolled in the VA health care program who would otherwise be placed in a nursing home facility.[3]

Respite care services were incorporated in an effort to assist family caregivers. As a result of the findings of the Caregiver Assistance Network which estimated that approximately 85 percent of all respite or home-care services in the United States dealt with spouses or adult children. The organization conducted a statewide survey in California that (1) indicated that at approximately 60 percent of family caregivers showed signs of clinical depression; and (2) that family members spent 11 hours or more caring for elderly family members. The Veteran's Millennium Health Care Act (VMHCA) gave the Department of Veteran's Affairs the authority to contract the needed services with community-based programs. The aim of the provision was to not only increase the quality of life for the caregiver, but to also increase the quality of life for the veteran by ensuring that the family caregiver was able to get some rest and return to care for the veteran in a less stressed or depressed state. The bill changed the entitlement of respite care from all eligible veterans to "enrolled" in the Veteran's Administration's health care system. Finally, in an effort to prepare for possible enrollment increases, Congress authorized the Department of Veteran's Affairs the right to contract out such services with community-based facilities.[4]

In addition, the legislation entitled veterans previously enrolled and receiving their primary health care benefits from VA operated facilities to home-health care visits in addition to non-institutional alternatives to nursing home care. This provision was included in an effort to ensure that veterans and their families were presented with alternatives to placing the veteran in a nursing home facility operated by the Veteran's Administration or state. Generally, veterans avoided or delayed entering a nursing home facility because it was the most expensive form of long-term health care. Therefore, the adding of non-institutional alternatives or providing for the means by which health care services can be in a home environment. Furthermore, the measure ensured that family caregivers in need of assistance would receive options that assisted them in maintaining their commitment to caring for the veteran. Congress concluded that by providing assistance and non-institutional options to home-caregivers, the Department of Veteran's Affairs could cut long-term care costs significantly.

Apart from the above, the Veteran's Millennium Health Care Act (VMHCA) required the Veteran's Administration to cover emergency care to veterans who lacked health care insurance coverage. Furthermore, presidential candidates in the 2000 election George W. Bush, Jr. and Vice-President Albert Gore supported the measure. In addition, Senators Arlen Specter, John Rockefeller, Olympia Snowe, Strom Thurmond and Representatives Stump, Stearns, Brown (FL), Smith (NJ), Evans articulated the importance of veteran's access to emergency care services. They maintained that reimbursing non-VA facilities for emergency care services was imperative to enhancing the quality of health care services administered by the Department of Veteran's Affairs. In 1999, before the passage of H.R. 2116, President William Jefferson Clinton suggested that every American should have access to emergency health care services. The president's stance on health care provided an impetus to supporters of veteran's health care.

Consequently, this provision ensured that veterans enrolled in the VA health care system who had no other means of paying for health care services were reimbursed for emergency treatment furnished by a non-VA hospital or health care provider. The Department of Veteran's Affairs was given the discretion of deciding the level of reimbursement. This measure required that the VA reimburse non-VA care providers with a "reasonable payment" comparable to that in the medical profession. Reimbursement was to be made directly to the health care provider, hospital, person, or organization that paid for the emergency treatment on behalf of the veteran. Therefore, the emergency care provision was significant because the Act ensured that veterans who relied solely on the Veteran's Administration's health care system could readily receive medical treatment in the case of an emergency.[5] Furthermore, the provision ensured that hospitals, organizations, individuals, or health care providers who rendered emergency treatment to veterans would be reimbursed for such services.[6]

Additionally, the Department of Veteran's Affairs was required to create a copayment policy for extended care treatment that exceeded 21 days in any given fiscal year. The copayment policy was applicable to veterans who were treated for non-compensible service connected disabilities. This policy also applied to veterans suffering from service-connected injuries whose income exceeded the allowed pension level. Consequently, the VA must establish a fund in the U.S. Treasury to deposit proceeds from copayments. These funds collected by the VA must then be used to expand extended care services in the facilities from which money was retrieved.[7] Title I, Subtitle B of the Veteran's Millennium Health Care Act (VMHCA) stipulated that veterans who "actively enrolled" in the Veteran's Administration health care system were entitled to reimbursement of emergency treatment of a "reasonable value". "Reasonable value" was defined as emergency care fees equal to fees charged by the VA for the same treatment. The term "actively enrolled" referred to veterans who were enrolled in the annual patient enrollment system or received hospital, nursing home care, or home care assistance under the veteran's health care program within the past 24 months. In addition, a third party (family member or organization) who paid for the emergency care services of veterans received outside of the VA system was entitled to reimbursement for a portion of the value of care provided, however, the responsibility to inform the department of payments made by a third party rested with the veteran. Furthermore, the department must report to Congress on the implementation of the emergency care reimbursement program for the fiscal years 2002 and 2003.[8]

Title I, Subtitle B, Section 102 of the statute required that the VA implement three pilot programs in an attempt to identify effective models of comprehensive health care delivery that would assist in reducing the use of hospital and nursing home care by elderly veterans. The first pilot program mandated that the VA provide services to eligible veterans by directly utilizing department operated facilities and personnel. The second program was required to provide health services to veterans through a combination of services provided by public and private health care providers and facilities with which the Department of Veteran's Affairs had contracts. The third pilot program is expected to meet the medical and health needs of veterans through a combination of services provided through cooperative agreements with appropriate public and private health care providers and VA facilities. These pilot programs were to be terminated in three years. The Department of Veteran's Affairs was required to report its findings to the House and Senate Veteran's Affairs Committees. This measure was incorporated into the final plan because Congress concluded that although the VA held expertise in the area of long-term health care, it failed to develop a health care system that focused on issues other than the current needs of veterans. It was the sentiment of members of the Veteran's Affairs Committee that the VA lacked the motivation to begin to develop a progressive health program that would address the future needs of the veteran's community. Therefore, Congress mandated that the Veteran's Administration should begin to collect data on cost-effective methods of providing quality long-term health care services.[9]

Apart from the above, the provision called on the Department of Veteran's Affairs to establish a pilot program for assisted-living services, permitted it to use its discretion to determine the region of the country where the program would be implemented, and authorized it to enter into contractual arrangements with the private sector for up to six months of assisted-living services for eligible veterans. The criteria for eligibility requires that the veteran must be eligible for placement assistance and must be determined to be unable to manage routine activities of daily living without supervision or assistance. Moreover, veterans who participated in this program were expected to remain in need of ongoing living assistance services following the termination of the program. Similar to the other pilot programs, the assisted-living program would expire three years after its inception. Furthermore, congressional oversight required the Secretary of the Department of Veteran's Affairs to submit a report to the House and Senate Veteran's Affairs Committees describing the manner in which the pilot program was implemented. The department must also compare the services rendered to veterans enrolled in the program with those rendered to seniors not enrolled in the program.[10] In addition, results of the program must be compared to home-care services provided by the department. When contracting services with non-VA service providers, the Department of Veteran's Affairs could only contract out services to facilities or caregivers that met the standards prescribed in Title 38, subsection 1730. Finally, if the department deemed it necessary to extend the assisted-living pilot program, it could make such a recommendation in the findings submitted to the two Veteran's Committees.

Title I, Subtitle B, Section 115 of the regulation expanded the counseling program to include individuals, primarily women, who had experienced sexual trauma. The provision called on the Veteran's Administration to provide counseling to the individuals in question through 2004. This law required that the department provide counseling and mental health services to veterans. It also ensured that information regarding counseling services and treatment was revised and updated in an attempt to increase program outreach efforts. As provided in the earlier parts of Sec. 102, the Department of Veteran's Affairs must submit to the Veteran's Affairs Committees in the House and Senate a status report on the program as well as the implementation of both the counseling outreach and sexual trauma programs. Lastly, both the Department of Veteran's Affairs and Department of Defense were required to present a joint report to Congress on their efforts to ensure that upon separation from military service, veterans were provided with current information about counseling and treatment programs, application procedures and eligibility requirements.[11]

The VMHCA also ordered the department to implement a program to enhance specialized mental health services available to veterans. The law placed particular emphasis on treatment of post-traumatic stress disorder and substance abuse disorders. Section 205 of the law amended the Veteran's health care Act of 1984 and reestablished the Committee on Post-Traumatic Stress Disorder. In addition, the Act required that $15 million be allocated to the department for the program. As an oversight requirement, the Department of Veteran's Affairs was required to report to Congress on the implementation of the specialized mental health program. This provision alone increased the department's funding level by $15 million over the previous spending level on mental health programs. The House and Senate Veteran's Affairs Committees further mandated that the Department of Veteran's Affairs report back to the committees within 12 months of the enactment of the new law, November 30, 1999, informing committee members about the methods it would used to implement the specialized mental health component of H.R. 2116. Congress and the President also mandated that the specialized mental health services be provided to veterans who were suffering from Post-Traumatic Stress Disorder caused by sexual abuse, sexual harassment, and chronic mental illness.[12]

The Veteran's Millennium Health Care Act (VHMCA) included a measure that ensures access to medical treatment in VA hospitals for veterans who served and received the Purple Heart Award. The Purple Heart medal is presented to veterans who were seriously injured during combat or were Prisoners-of-War (POWs). Congress estimated that there were approximately 250,000 awardees then suffering from service-connected disabilities. It, therefore, mandated that the Department of Veteran's Affairs should give such veterans priority in receiving medical, hospital, and nursing home care.[13]

Title I, Section 113 of the law directed the Department of Defense and the Department of Veteran's Affairs to enter into an agreement that required the Veteran's Administration to provide reimbursement fees to military retirees who were eligible for health care services under TRICARE, the Department of Defense's managed health care program. Both agencies must reach an agreement within nine months following the enactment of the Act. Finally, Congress mandated that the Department of Defense include in subsequent TRICARE contracts provisions to implement the agreement reached with the Department of Veteran's Affairs.[14]

Title II of the Veteran's Millennium Health Care Act (VMHCA) gave the Department of Veteran's Affairs the authority to increase veteran's co-payments for non-service connected disabilities or conditions. Prior to the enactment of the Act, a copayment of $2 was required for a 30-day supply of medication. The new law allowed the department to establish its own maximum monthly and annual co-payment ceilings for veterans who received multiple outpatient prescriptions. The provision also allowed the Veteran's Administration (VA) to increase veteran's copayments for health care services administered by the Department of Veteran's Affairs for non-service connected illness. The measure, further, allowed the Department to adjust copayment fees for veterans with higher income levels.[15]

Although both the Democratic and Republican parties acknowledged that veterans would have a difficult time paying the increased copayments, the Republican leadership nevertheless argued that it was necessary to include such a provision in the bill because it was convinced that was the only tangible means by which the Department of Veteran's Affairs would be able to: (1) increase veteran's access to comprehensive health care services and (2) assist the department in becoming less dependent on federal dollars for providing medical services to veterans. The rationale behind increasing copayments was that the VA would be required to provide more services and veterans would have to pay more in order to have increased access to comprehensive health care services. Furthermore, the Republican leadership maintained that increasing copayments would facilitate the department to raise additional revenue and become less dependent on budget allocations.[16]

Title II of the law required the Veteran's Administration to collect copayments and deposit them into a fund in the Department of Treasury. All revenue collected must be redistributed to the facility from which it was recovered. The statute mandated the VA to monitor and evaluate the health status of the dependents of veterans who served in the Persian Gulf War. The VA must compile a report that focused on their health status through December 2003. Furthermore, the Veteran's Administration (VA) was required to reestablish a committee to study and evaluate Post-Traumatic Stress Disorder (PTSD). The effects of PTSD can be as severe as to cause paranoia or an inability to maintain employment due to psychological stress[17]

Title II, Section 202 established the Department of Veteran's Affairs Health Improvement Fund within the Department of Treasury. The deposits were to be used for the improvement of various veteran's health care services.[18] In addition, the law allowed funds from the Department of Veteran's Affairs Medical Care Collections Fund to be channeled to VA facilities. It should be reiterated that under the previous law, the department could only distribute funds to each designated region. Additionally, Section 204 of Title II revised several provisions of the bill relating to non-profit research corporations at VA medical centers. Therefore, nonprofit research corporations were authorized to provide education and training to Veteran's Health

Administration health care personnel. The Act further required non-profit research corporations to enlarge its board of directors in order to ensure that the veteran's community was represented on it. In addition, the Act prohibited non-profit research corporations from expending funds for an education activity before receiving the approval of the Department's Under Secretary of Health.[19]

Title IV of the VMHCA addressed issues concerning construction and maintenance of facilities and hospitals operated by the Department of Veteran's Affairs. The Act revised the priority system for awarding grants to State home construction grant program. The law placed priority on grant applications for renovation projects; highest priority was given to those plans that were aimed at remedying existing safety problems. In addition, preference was given to those proposals that emphasized increasing the availability of hospital beds. Thus, those States that operated veteran's nursing homes were given priority over those applications that exhibited only a moderate or limited need for bed space. The Statute modified the manner in which construction contracts were awarded (emphasis is currently placed on renovating already existing VA health care facilities and hospitals). While, the measure protected the interests of states that submitted grant applications in the 2000 award period, state homes would be required to adhere to the new criteria beginning fiscal year 2001. Under the new law, the Department of Veteran's Affairs was given greater discretion to close old and obsolete or underused VA medical facilities. Thus, priority could be given to grant proposals in which states and agencies submit plans to build new medical facilities.[20] Additionally, the new policy expanded VA's authority to enter into long-term lease agreements with "property-owners" to improve its health care delivery system. The Act extended the duration of lease agreements for up to 75 years. Funds collected from these contractual agreements were to be deposited into a Health Services Improvement Fund. These monies will later be used to enhance the delivery of medical treatment to veterans.

Under Title II of the statute, the VMHCA covered an assortment of medical conditions. For example, the law forced the VA to report any plans to reduce available space in VA operated facilities by more than 50 percent. The Veteran's Administration was, further required to consult with chiropractors to provide chiropractic treatment to veterans. Finally, this section of the law renamed the "Ionnis

Lougaris" medical center located in Reno, Nevada the "Jack Streeter Building."[21]

Title IV, Section 401 of the law authorized the Department of Veteran's Affairs to build new medical facilities in Lebanon, Pennsylvania; Atlanta, Georgia; Fargo, North Dakota; Kansas City, Missouri; Orlando, Florida and Leavenworth, Kansas. Title IV also allowed the Veteran's Administration to enter into leases for medical facilities in San Diego, California and Lubbock, Texas.[22] In order to bring the preceding into reality, Congress authorized federal appropriations for fiscal years 2000 and 2001 for major facility renovation projects and the construction of new VA facilities. It appropriated $14,500,000 for the construction of the long-term care facility to be created at the Department of Veteran's Affairs medical facility in Lebanon, Pennsylvania while providing $13,000,000 for the construction of a surgical suite and post-anesthesia care unit at the VA facility in Kansas City, Missouri. Congress also appropriated $5,600,000 for the demolition of buildings located at the Dwight D. Eisenhower Department of Veteran's Affairs Medical Center in Leavenworth, Kansas.[23]

In addition, to the above, the Veteran's Millennium Health Care Act (VMHCA) authorized the Veteran's Administration (VA) to conduct renovations and environmental improvements to the VA medical facility in Fargo, North Dakota. An amount of $12,000,000 was allocated for the renovation project. The Act also authorized $12, 400,000 for a renovation project in Atlanta, Georgia. Lastly, the legislation provided the amount of $2,4000,000 for the renovation of a domiciliary or home care facility in Orlando, Florida. The funds authorized for the Orlando renovation project were taken from those previously appropriated for major construction and renovation projects prior to fiscal year 2000.[24] The statute also directed the Department of Veteran's Affairs to lease an outpatient clinic in Lubbock, Texas. Congress funded the project at $1,112,000. The new law further required the Department of Veteran's Affairs to lease a research facility in San Diego, California with the stipulation that the cost must exceed $1,066,5000. [25]

Title V, Subtitle A, Section 501 of the Act provided payment of Dependency and Indemnity Compensation (DIC) to the surviving spouse of a former Prisoner-of-War (POW). In order for the spouse to receive DIC, the veteran must have been determined by the Department of Veteran's Affairs to have been completely disabled at the time of death. Furthermore, the bill noted that the remarriage of a surviving spouse should not automatically bar one from benefits. However, if the department determines that the marriage ended in divorce due to fraud or collusion, the department would not obligated to provide a surviving spouse with dependency and Indemnity compensation (DIC). Equally important, section 501 noted that the department was not required to provide housing loans or educational assistance to a surviving spouse if the marriage ended due to fraud committed against the veteran.[26]

Title VI, Subtitle A of the Veteran's Millennium Health Care Act (VMHCA) directed the American Battle Monuments Commission to solicit and accept contributions for establishing the World War II memorial in the District of Columbia or the DC metropolitan area. The Department of Treasury created a fund to receive and expend contributions made toward the construction of such a memorial. The American Battle Monuments Commission was allowed to borrow up to $65 million from the Department of Treasury to ensure that the groundbreaking, construction, and dedication of the site were completed in a timely fashion. It is important to note that the groundbreaking for the World War II Memorial took place on Veteran's Day - November 11, 2000. The Commission was also permitted to accept voluntary services in an effort to facilitate fundraising for the project. The Act authorized the Commission to reimburse volunteers for incidental expenses. The time allotted for the construction of the completed memorial was extended from May 25, 2000 to December 31, 2005.[27] In addition, the new law allowed the Commission to receive donations or contributions for the World War II memorial from State, local and private entities. In this connection, Congress authorized the World War II Memorial to solicit contributions and mandated that donations be deposited in a separate account earmarked for the World War II Memorial. Furthermore, the American Battle Monuments Commission was required to formulate written guidelines and regulations under which contributions to the memorial were to be accepted.

The Act likewise required the Veteran's Administration to make medical coverage available to veterans suffering from bronchiolo alveolar carcinoma. This illness is said to be caused by the inhalation of atomic particles. It affects the tiny branches in the air tubes and sacs of the lung, which are located at the end of the bronchioles or airways of the lung. The disease affects one's ability to carry air from the mouth to the air sacs in the lungs. The cancer causes an inflammation of the bronchioles -- air sac -- of individuals suffering from it. Prior to this new law, the Department of Veteran's Affairs did not consider this form of cancer as one that should be covered under the veteran's health care program. The legislation forced the department to add it to its list of radiogenic cancers. As a result, the department was forced to recognize bronchiolo alveolar carcinoma as a service-connected disease. Therefore, veterans suffering with this form of cancer were required to obtain medical treatment outside of the Veteran's Administration's health care system. This provision in the law is significant because it forced a shift in the department's policy and required that the Veteran's Administration provide medical treatment for veterans who were exposed to atomic materials during their military service. Based on these facts, Congress was determined that veterans who came in contact with atomic materials during their service in the United States military were entitled to VA health care.[28]

Furthermore, the Act gave the VA the authority to establish six additional veteran's cemeteries. Although the law did not specify where the cemeteries were to be located, Congress did suggest that the VA should consider establishing them in Atlanta, Miami, Oklahoma City, Pittsburgh, Detroit, and Sacramento, California. The recommendations were made because burial space was extremely limited in these regions of the United States. Additionally, the Act (VMHCA) extended the operation of the Santa Fe National Cemetery in New Mexico. Congress was determined to ensure that, at the very least, the government had an obligation to ensure that national cemeteries were available for the burial of veterans. The Santa Fe National Cemetery was expected to run out of burial space by the end of fiscal year 2000. The VMHCA required the Department of Veteran's Affairs to allow flat grave makers to be utilized in an effort to extend the viability and operation of the national cemetery. Hence, the department was forced to change its policy of only allowing upright grave headstones in national cemeteries. This measure is significant because not only did it extend the viability of the Santa Fe National Cemetery through fiscal year 2008, the measure inevitably extended the lifespan of national cemeteries by determining a way to maximize the utilization of burial space.[29] Congress, in addition, directed the department to conduct an independent study on its efforts to improve the condition of existing cemeteries.

Title VII of the directive amended federal veteran's educational benefits. The provision authorized the use of educational benefits to prepare veterans who were willing to test for admission into colleges and graduate programs. Section 702 extended eligibility for basic educational assistance benefits under the Montgomery "GI" Bill for individuals who were discharged from the military. In addition, H.R. 2116 directed the department to report to the House and Senate Committee on Veteran's Affairs efforts to improve the veteran's education and vocational training benefits. Moreover, Subtitle B of Title VII extended the eligibility for housing loans to veterans who had served in the "Selected Reserve." The program date was extended from September 30, 2003 to September 30, 2007.[30]

Under Title VIII of the Act, the Department of Veteran's Affairs was required to implement a quality assurance program within the Veteran's Benefits Administration. The department was given the discretion to determine whether it was appropriate to create an individual department or separate quality assurance entities. This new mandate ordered the Under-Secretary for Benefits at the Veteran's Administration to implement and oversee quality reviews of the organizational components recognized by the Administration. This was aimed at ensuring improved management of the program. Additionally, the department was asked to present an annual report to Congress stating the methods and means employed to facilitate or increase quality assurance. Moreover, H.R. 2116 extended both the Advisory Committee on Minority Veterans and the department's authority to maintain a region office in the Republic of the Philippines.[31]

Title IX instructed the department to reintegrate homeless veterans into the labor force. The Homeless Veteran's Reintegration Program would be implemented through grants, contracts or services provided directly by the Veteran's Administration. The VA would use the grants to purchase vans to increase program outreach to homeless veterans. In addition, as an oversight measure, Congress asked the department to work with both the Department of Labor and Department of Housing and Urban Development to create a detailed plan for evaluating the effectiveness of its homeless veteran's program.[32]

Under Title II, Subtitle A, Section 203, Congress established the Veteran's Health Services Improvement Fund. Congress did so to ensure that if a lawsuit was brought against tobacco manufacturers by the United States federal government all settlement proceeds will be deposited into the account. Therefore, the Department of Veteran's Affairs, if it so decided could file a lawsuit against tobacco manufacturers for costs incurred in treating veterans with tobacco related illnesses, i.e. respiratory problems and lung cancer. In such instances, tobacco settlement funds would be used to (1) furnish medical care and (2) conduct medical and rehabilitative health systems research. Special emphasis was placed on medical research that addressed issues of prevention, and treatment or rehabilitation of diseases associated with tobacco use.[33]

The comprehensive veteran's package also addressed the retirement and survivor annuity program available to judges who served on the U.S. Court of Appeals for Veteran's Claims. The law instituted a "staggered" retirement policy ensure that as justices retire, the court would have sufficient personnel to carry out the business of the court. The retirement program is now consistent with programs that cover federal judges.[34] Furthermore, the Act spelled out the terms for the early retirement of current judges. A judge is eligible to retire early if he or she has served at least 10 years of "credible" service within the U.S. Court of Appeals for Veteran's Claims. Judges who have served 20 years on the court and are 55 years or older could notify the Department of Veteran's Affairs of his or her intent to retire.[35] In addition, the statute modified the terms under which two new judges would be appointed to the Court. It limited the tenure of judges by stipulating that they could not serve more than 13 years. Judges would be required to retire following 13 years of service on the Court. However, Title X, Section 1021, subsection 7257 stipulated that a retired judge may be recalled to serve on the court. Upon retirement, each justice would be required to submit in writing a notice to the Chief Justice of the Court if he or she desires to be recalled for future service. This provision allowed the Chief Justice to allow former justices to return to the Court. A judge once called out of retirement to serve on the Court, according to the statute, could not refuse. He or she could not serve on the Court for more than 90 days in any given calendar year. In instances where the Chief Justice would want a judge to serve more than 90 days, the judge must consent. When a justice is recalled and declines to carryout his or her duties, the Chief Justice retains the authority to either remove the judge's name from the list of "recall-eligible" judges. recall list or recall the judge at another time.[36] Apart from this, the "recalled judge" must fully perform his or her responsibilities just as a regular judge and receive a salary commensurate to an active judge less his/her retirement annuity. Hence, the retirement annuity would be subtracted from the current salary of the justice to determine compensation for returning to the Court.[37]

Lastly, under the new law the VA offered employees incentives (buyouts) to voluntarily retire from the department (these early retirement packages offered as much as $25,000).[38] The Department of Veteran's Affairs hopes to streamline the remaining positions and thereby increase the overall efficiency of the Veteran's Administration (VA).

Conclusion

The Veteran's Millennium Health Care Act (VMHCA) is the first comprehensive veteran's reform bill enacted in more than twenty years. Representative Stearns introduced the bill in the 106th Congress on June 9, 1999. The American Legion formulated the original draft legislation.[39] However, the structure and legislative measures included in the bill signed by President Clinton was significantly different from the draft proposal.

Public Law 106-117 consisted of more than 70 provisions, many of which were introduced independently of the Veteran's Millennium Health Care Act (VHMCA), by Representative Christopher Smith, Representative Stump, Senator Charles Robb, and Senator Arlen Specter. The provisions became a part of the legislated comprehensive package.

The House and Senate Veteran's Affairs Committees had failed to act on the legislative proposals that were added to the comprehensive veteran's bill. In fact, had the Republican and Democratic leaderships not acted in a bi-partisan fashion, it is likely that many of the legislative proposals introduced would not have become a part of the Veteran's Millennium Health Care Act (VMHCA). Prior to the passage of the VMHCA, Congress addressed veteran's issues in a piecemeal fashion.

The comprehensive veteran's bill attempted to redress many of the inherent problems plaguing the Department of Veteran's Affairs and the implementation of veteran's entitlement programs. The Act (VMHCA) of 1999 is significant because it reformed major aspects of the veteran's health care system and other veteran's benefits by doing the following:

1. extended the housing loan program from fiscal year 2003-2007; the program offers home loans for members of reserve components with at least six (6) years service

2. authorized the VA to pay for emergency care costs of veterans who were receiving their medical treatment through the administration
3. permitted veterans to use money from the Montgomery GI Bill to pay for courses to prepare them for the Scholastic Aptitude Test (SAT) or Graduate Record Examination (GRE)
4. mandated the Veteran's Administration (VA) to provide medical care to military retirees enrolled in the Department of Defense's TRICARE program
5. required the VA to offer priority care to veterans who were recipients of the Purple Heart Award
6. added bronchiolo alveolar carcinoma, a rare form of lung cancer to the VA's list of service-connected diseases
7. directed the Department of Veteran's Affairs to create six new national cemeteries
8. extended the viability of national cemeteries and burial benefits to veterans who wished to be laid to rest in such a cemetery
9. protected the interests of intergovernmental agencies and administrators that operate State veteran's homes by ensuring that grant proposals for fiscal year 2000 were awarded based on the previous criteria which gave preference to renovation projects as opposed to organizations which wanted to build new medical facilities and nursing homes
10. ordered the creation of a memorial for World-War II veterans
11. allowed the American Battle Monuments Commission to borrow $65 million from the U.S. Treasury; this would help finance the ground breaking and secure a location for the World-War II Memorial
12. increased veteran's access to chiropractic services
13. increased veteran's access to psychological counseling treatment for Post-Traumatic Stress Disorder (PTSD), sexual abuse and trauma, alcohol and drug abuse, etc....

Public Law 106-117 also offered enhanced educational benefits to veterans. The Department of Veteran's Affairs was hopeful that expanding educational opportunities would result in fewer veterans becoming dependent on the VA health care system for medical treatment. Although the law specified that veterans should receive increased access to quality medical services, emergency care treatment, education programs, etc., it all depends on how the law is implemented.

Notes

[1]The House appointed Representatives Stump, Evans, Stearns, Quinn , Brown, and Doyle to the conference committee. Senate conferees included: Senators Specter, Rockefeller, and Thurmond.

[2] U.S. Congress, House and Senate, Joint Committee on Veteran's Affairs, *The Veteran's Millennium Health Care Act*, Conference Report 106-470, 106th Cong., 1st sess., 19 November 1999, 10-11.

[3] Ibid.

[4] Ibid., 10-12.

[5]U.S. Congress, Senator Arlen Spector of Pennsylvania speaking for the Veteran's Millennium Health Care Act: H.R. 2116, 106th Cong., 1st sess., Congressional Record, 19 November 1999, S14904.

[6] U.S. Congress, House and Senate, Joint Committee on Veteran's Affairs, *The Veteran's Millennium Health Care Act*, Conference Report 106-470, 106th Cong., 1st sess., 19 November 1999, 13-16.

[7] Ibid., 20.

[8] Ibid., 10-12.

[9] Ibid.

[10] Ibid., 11-12.

[11] Ibid., 18-19.

[12] Ibid., 19-20.

[13] Ibid., 16-17.

[14] Ibid., 16.

[15] Ibid., 20-31.

[16] Ibid.

[17] Ibid., 24-25.

[18] Ibid., 21.

[19] Ibid., 22-24.

[20] Ibid., 34-36.

[21] Ibid., 34.

[22] Ibid., 34.

[23] Ibid., 35.

[24] Ibid.

[25] Ibid.

[26] Ibid., 35-36.

[27] Ibid., 38-42.

[28] Ibid., 37.

[29] Ibid., 3.

[30] Ibid., 45.

[31] Ibid., 47-49.

[32] Ibid., 49-50.

[33] Ibid., 21.

---

[34] Ibid., 51-53.

[35] Ibid.

[36] Ibid., 54-55.

[37] Ibid.

[38] Ibid.

[39]Steve Robertson, 28 November 2000. The personal (e-mail) communication from Mr. Robertson, Director of the National Legislative Council for the American Legion.

CHAPTER 6

CONCLUSION

The purpose of this dissertation was to examine the saliency of partisanship in the U.S. Congress, on issues of national significance. Specifically, the study treats the behavior and activities utilized by members of Congress, interest groups, and the executive branch to shape and influence the passage of the comprehensive veteran's legislation - the Veteran's Millennium Health Care Act of 1999. Malcolm Jewell and Samuel Patterson's "Legislative Configuration System" and the "Legislative Role Orientations" Model were employed throughout this study.

Jewell and Patterson's "Legislative Configuration System" model provided the fundamental theoretical framework for observing the political actors' involvement in the formulation and the enactment of the veteran's bill. This model delineates between internal and external factors that affect the legislative process. In addition to the "Legislative Configuration System," the "Legislative Role Orientations Model" made it possible to investigate the relationships or connection between the participants -- members of Congress, the Chief Executive, interest groups, administrative agencies, and bureaucrats, and public opinion. This model was invaluable in assisting the author in identifying and understanding the behavior of key individuals and groups outside of the legislative system. The "Legislative Orientations

Model" also made it possible to observe the interactions of these groups with one another.

Therefore, the author maintains that in order to comprehend the passage of the Veteran's Millennium Health Care Act (VMHCA), which attempts to redress a number of problems plaguing the veteran's health care system and other veteran's benefits, it is crucial to differentiate between the roles assumed by the participants. Jewell and Patterson's models helped facilitate studying the participants and the roles they play in the legislative process, thereby allowing the goals of this study to be met. An effort was made throughout this research paper to investigate the activities used by each participant. This study also made an effort to investigate the interactions various participants had with one another during the consideration and passage of the Veteran's Millennium Health Care Act.

The Role of the President

President William Jefferson Clinton utilized several techniques to influence the enactment of the "Veteran's Millennium Health Care Act of 1999." The president used his role as "chief legislator" to voice his opinion on veteran's health care in the United States. He also relied on his political skills to persuade, negotiate and compromise with members of Congress. President Clinton traveled the country making public appeals for health care reform. The president shared his views on veteran's health care and benefits with Congress and the American public when he addressed the nation in State of the Union Addresses and weekly radio addresses. Additionally, he made numerous appearances before veteran's groups in which he indicated his support for reforming the VA benefits system. All this occurred against the backdrop of a highly partisan impeachment process that threatened to remove him from office.

Furthermore, President Clinton's key cabinet officials such as William Cohen, Secretary of the Department of Defense (DOD) communicated the administration's policy position with interest groups and state agencies. Finally, President Clinton used his "bureaucracy" - key bureaucrats (e.g. Under Secretary for the Department of Veteran's Affairs and Stephen Backhus, Director of Veteran's Medical Health Care and Issues) as a tool to influence the legislative process and the passage of the 1999 veteran's legislation.

Due to the non-controversial nature of the veteran's health care issues, the president did not resort to "arm-twisting" or threats to veto legislation. In order to narrow differences on veteran's health care, the president relied on executive officials such as Kenneth Kizer and Stephen Backhus to articulate the administration's position on the provisions of the Act. The president did not propose any provisions that were diametrically opposed to the bi-partisan plan. Most importantly, President Clinton used his bureaucracy to interact with Congress and veteran's interest groups. Stephen Backhus and Kenneth Kizer played an integral role as members of the Clinton administration. Both Kizer and Backhus testified at several congressional hearings on strategic planning and budgeting within the Department of Veteran's Affairs and the Veteran's Millennium Health Care Act (VMHCA) of 1999.

The Role of Interest Groups

Public opinion and interest groups were integral in influencing the shaping and passage of the Veteran's Millennium Health Care Act (VMHCA). Although public opinion polls were not conducted to measure public support for VMHCA, the public has consistently supported the provision of veteran's benefits by the United States government. This is evident in public opinion data from 1947 to 1999 discussed in Chapter Four.

In addition, interest groups were also instrumental in the development and passage of the Act. Among those who participated in the creation of House bill H.R. 2116 were veteran's groups, government interest groups and managed care organizations. These groups engaged in grassroots lobbying, coalition building, and lobbying the national legislature. Veteran's groups (e.g., the American Legion, Vietnam Veterans of America, Veterans of Foreign Wars, Jewish War Veterans and Paralyzed Veterans of America) worked cooperatively to pressure the legislature and the President to further expand veteran's entitlements.

Likewise, government interest groups participated in shaping the bill. There was primarily one government group, the State Veteran's Homes Association, involved in facilitating the passage of the Act. The organization worked on building coalitions with veteran's organizations. The group, like veteran's groups, testified before the House and Senate Veteran's Affairs Committees. Each of the interest groups involved in the development of the legislation relied on communicating with Congress and President Clinton through use of conferences, national conventions, grassroots lobbying efforts, and testifying in congressional hearings. The coalition that existed between these groups was formed around a one primary objective, improving veteran's health care and benefits. This approach helped ensure the passage of House bill H.R. 2116 - The Veteran's Millennium Health Care Act of 1999.

The Role of Political Parties

Party cohesion was not an influential factor in the passage of the Veteran's Millennium Health Care Act of 1999. Essentially, both Republicans and Democrats set aside their ideological differences in order that they might "fast-track" the passage of the bill. During the first session of the 106th Congress, House Republican Cliff Stearns (R-FL) unveiled his legislative plan to expand veteran's benefits and to improve the delivery of VA services to veterans. The original legislation included a series of legislative measures aimed at strengthening veteran's programs. Representative Lane Evans (D-IL), ranking member of the Committee on Veteran's Affairs, joined with Stearns to support the reform package. The willingness displayed by Stearns and Evans prompted rank-and-file members of both parties to join in the "spirit of bipartisan cooperation." Consequently, Republicans and Democrats combined their efforts to improve veteran's entitlements. This was a clever political strategy. Essentially, this approach helped ensure the passage of the Veteran's Millennium Health Care Act.

However, there was some disagreement on increasing fees charged to veterans for treatment provided by the Veteran's Administration. Democrats believed that increases in veteran's co-payments would place an unfair burden on those who were experiencing difficulty paying. Nevertheless, GOP leaders decided to keep the measure. They argued the increases were necessary to offset the cost of implementing the expanded health care program.

Members also introduced language aimed at reforming veteran's benefits. Several measures were introduced before the drafting of House bill H.R. 2116. Thus, the bipartisan approach to the bill proved beneficial for all involved. Members were given the opportunity to have pending legislation incorporated into the legislative proposal. Moreover, the cooperative and swift action on the part of

Congress produced an opportunity for virtually every member of Congress to claim credit for its passage. Hence, the passage of the VMHCA created a chance for Republicans and Democrats to claim credit for the new law during the 2000 congressional elections.

In addition, both parties discussed the bill with President Clinton. The president extended his support to congressional leadership on reforming veteran's health care. Essentially, several health care reform measures proposed by the President and First Lady Hillary Clinton in 1992 were included in the Veteran's Millennium Health Care Act (VMHCA). Although the president indicated his support for the Act, the majority of negotiations took place between members of Congress and the Department of Veteran's Affairs.

This paper examined the legislative process through the lens of the Veteran's Millennium Health Care Act (VMHCA) of 1999. The investigation into the formulation and enactment of the veteran's reform law was influenced by a number of participants, i.e., veteran's interest groups, members of Congress, the president and executive officials, intergovernmental agencies and health care professionals. The paradigms developed by Malcolm Jewell and Samuel Patterson were utilized to investigate the interactions between participants and the legislative system.[1] The "Legislative Role Orientations Model" provided a theoretical framework for assessing the roles played by legislators. This study indicates that there were a variety of interactions between the president, interest groups, and congressional committees in attempting to shape and promote the passage of the veteran's bill. Although, each participant was successful in their own right, they had to negotiate on a few provisions like increases in veteran's co-payments in order to ensure the success of the legislative proposal. While the legislation was heavily influenced by years of lobbying by veteran's organizations, a number of actors shared in shaping the direction of the modified veteran's benefits policy. Consequently, the final legislative product was influenced by a variety of interactions between external actors and the members of the legislature. The relationships between all those involved were supportive and facilitated the passage and enactment of the Veteran's Millennium Health Care Act (VMHCA). Furthermore, legislators assumed a number of roles orientations in the passage of the VMHCA. The designers of the paradigms used throughout this study suggest that these role orientations emerge among legislators who intermingle with participants within the legislative system. Through examining the interaction of members of Congress and participants involved in the passage of the veteran's bill, the author was able to identify several role orientations assumed by legislators. The role orientation of both Republican and Democratic members of Congress was "non-executive" in nature. Much of their interaction with representatives of the Department of Veteran's Affairs hinged on the "agency-oriented" role orientation of legislators. However, their interaction with the Department of Veteran's Affairs can be seen as being "executive-oriented" since the department indirectly articulates the desires of the president's. Consequently, the desires of the president were largely communicated through the interaction between Congress and top bureaucrats from the Veteran's Administration (VA). Because the legislative proposal was bi-partisan in nature, the author contends that legislators from both the majority and minority parties assumed the role orientation of either "party-man" or "party indifferent/party-man." Additionally, legislators behaved in a manner that facilitated the legislative goals and objectives of interest groups, especially veteran's organizations. As such, the interest group role orientation of members of Congress was as "facilitator" in their dealings with neutral groups like the American Legion and the American Health Care Association. In fact, there exists virtually no evidence that legislators behaved in the "resister" role orientation in their dealings with interest groups and bureaucrats. In fact, the majority of those involved participated in a manner that promoted a "spirit of bipartisanship." It was precisely this spirit that enabled the Veteran's Millennium Health Care Act (VMHCA) to be enacted within five months of being introduced in Congress.

The main findings of this dissertation are that there exist several distinctive roles and patterns of interactions that allowed legislators to proceed with the veteran's reform bill in a comprehensive and bipartisan manner, even within a larger political climate that was among the most partisan in the history of the country. The role orientations observed are as follows: (1) the "agency-oriented" role orientation members of Congress demonstrated towards officials from the Department of Veteran's Affairs made it possible for VA officials to promote their legislative goals under the guise of the Democratic Party; (2) President Clinton articulated his overwhelming support for United States veterans; (3) the "facilitator" role orientation exhibited by interest groups promoted the goal of veteran's organizations like the American Legion which contributed to the drafting of the original legislation ; (4) legislators assumed the "politico" role orientation in their drafting and treatment the veteran's bill role of a "politico" member; (5) the bi-partisan nature of the Act and the "non-partisan" role orientation of Republicans and Democrats coupled with institutional support from groups like American Health Care Association (AHCA) helped guarantee the passage of veteran's reform legislation; (6) the support displayed for the subcommittee chairs' proposal and the spirit of bi-partisanship between the parties made it possible for congressional leaders to pass the comprehensive legislative proposal; (7) the rank-and-file members of the legislature assumed the "ritualist" role orientation in their favorable acceptance of the recommendation of the House and Senate Veteran's Affairs Committee; and (9) the majority of rank-and-file members also behaved as "opportunist" and used the time allotted for debate to declare their "patriotism" and unending support for American veterans.

The Interactions of the President and the "Executive Role" and "Bureaucratic Role" Orientations of Legislators

It is the contention of the writer that President William Jefferson Clinton played a very important role in influencing the 1999 veteran's bill. Health care reform was the cornerstone of the president's 1992 presidential election platform. Following attacks by the Republican Party and interest groups like health care professionals and health insurance companies, Clinton's universal health care plan was demolished. Therefore, it was important that the president to get as many of his health care reform proposals included in the veteran's health care and benefits reform legislation. In 1999, President Clinton faced a less challenging task to get the Republican leadership to embrace his proposals. In an effort to influence the GOP majority in the 106th Congress, the president communicated with Congress, the American public, his bureaucracy, and interest groups.

In order to impress upon the legislature the need for veteran's health care and benefit reforms, the Chief Executive communicated with these groups through presidential weekly addresses, State of the Union Addresses, Veteran's Day speeches, and health care conferences. As a result, the Chief Executive was able to influence public opinion on improving veteran's entitlement programs. It was the president, who urged challenged the Republican majority Congress and Democratic membership to work in a cooperative manner to pass a bi-partisan veteran's reform bill. In speeches to interest groups, he advocated expanding long-term health care, reimbursing veterans for emergency health care services, increasing access to VA medical treatment facilities, and improving the quality of VA services.

It is this writer's opinion that President Clinton's proposal helped facilitate efforts to reform Veteran's programs. Although, he did not offer a comprehensive proposal, he supplied several key legislative measures that were incorporated in the Veteran's Millennium Health Care Act (VMHCA). Whether intended or not, Clinton used legislation to maintain an environment of bipartisanship that inhibited further partisan alienation from Republicans that may have resulted in his being removed from office.

Furthermore, the bureaucratic role orientations of the GOP controlled 106th Congress exhibited both an "executive role" orientation and an "agency role orientation. The Republican controlled legislature did not act as spokespersons for President Clinton. However, the bi-partisan nature of the bill afforded Democratic leadership the opportunity to act as spokespersons for the president. As such, the GOP majority indirectly aided president Clinton in achieving several of his veteran's health care policy objectives.

In addition, the GOP controlled Congress was executive oriented in accommodating Clinton's policy preferences, including emergency health care reimbursement, long-term care and quality health care mechanisms. Clearly, the executive role orientations of Democratic members were executive oriented. They introduced legislation that helped fulfill President Clinton's policy recommendations.

In conclusion, while the Executive lacked a comprehensive plan, Clinton's legislative agenda provided a foundation for developing the Veteran's Millennium Health Care Act. This approach to veteran's health care reform indirectly allowed the president to fulfill several of his health care reform goals. Thus, the executive oriented legislature and exhibition of bi-partisan cooperation facilitated the passage of the 1999 veteran's bill.

Public Opinion and Interest Groups and the "Facilitator" Role Orientations of Legislators

Public opinion and interest groups were instrumental in influencing the passage of the veteran's reform bill. Public response to the plight of veterans is heavily linked to public opinion polls.

Although the polling data failed to specifically address the Veteran's Millennium Health Care Act, public opinion has consistently been supportive of strengthening and expanding veteran's entitlement programs. From as early as the late 1940s, it has been evident that the public supported increasing veteran's benefits, i.e., pensions, home loans, education loans, health care services, and preferential treatment in employment. Seemingly, positive public opinion and America's reverence towards veterans made it possible for Republican and Democratic members of Congress to join forces to improve the veteran's health care delivery system. Before this comprehensive bill, Congress had addressed issues confronting the veteran's community in a piecemeal fashion.

Interest groups played a role in the enactment of the 1999 veteran's legislation. They played a significant role in the shaping of the Veteran's Millennium Health Care Act (VMHCA) through their interaction with Congress and President William Jefferson Clinton. Many of the interest groups communicated their perspective on the legislation through phone calls, letters, faxes and conferences and congressional hearings. President Clinton articulated his support and respect for veterans on a number of occasions. Furthermore, the veteran's health care reform bill received the president's support. This was largely due to the sense of indebtedness the country feels for their sacrifices and military service. Moreover, several health care provisions were incorporated from President Clinton's 1992 health care reform plan. Hence, in light of the state of long-term care nationally, the legislation received the president's endorsement.

Both Republican and Democratic leadership were receptive to the demands of all the interest groups involved in shaping the veteran's bill. This receptiveness is represented by the fact that the House and Senate Committees on Veteran's Affairs schedule annually legislative hearing for veteran's issues. During these hearings, veteran's groups are able to articulate their legislative agenda to Congress. The rank-and-file membership also facilitated the passage of the Veteran's Millennium Health Care Act (VMHCA). They embraced the legislative proposal formulated by the Veteran's Affairs Committee in both chambers. The unwavering support received by the GOP Congress for the bi-partisan legislation enabled legislators on both sides of the isles to advance their legislative agenda. In conclusion, the consistent support enabled members of Congress to pass the first comprehensive veteran's bill in over twenty years.

In addition, public opinion indicated a reverence for veterans. Public opinion heavily supported expanding veteran's benefits. Undoubtedly, public opinion helped promote the legislative agenda articulated by veteran's interest groups, and health care administrators and professionals. Among the interest groups involved were veteran's organizations, governmental interest groups, and private interest groups. The veteran's interest groups built coalitions with one another and with state governmental interest groups (e.g., National Association of State Nursing Homes). Veteran's organizations (such as the American Legion, Non-Commissioned Officers of America, Vietnam Veterans of America, Jewish War Veterans, and Paralyzed Veterans of America) all banned together in order to strengthen their position on veteran's health care issues. The coalition tactic or strategy assisted in solidifying claims made by the veteran's community for increased benefits. These groups also communicated with the executive branch, i.e., the president and executive officials, in an effort to further influence public policy. Veteran's organizations issued statements to Congress and testified at congressional hearings on veteran's health care issues and the Veteran's Millennium Health Care Act (VMHCA). These groups also organized meetings with members of Congress and members of the House and Senate Committees on Veteran's Affairs.

One group in particular, the American Legion played a crucial role in the formulation and shaping of the Act. Many of the group's recommendations were incorporated into the veteran's bill. In fact, the Legion authored the original draft legislation for Representative Cliff Stearns (R-FL). Furthermore, the American Legion used grassroots lobbying, newsletters and mailings to inform its more than 2,500,000 members of its efforts to secure expanded VA services for veterans. The organization heavily promoted its legislative agenda for increased access to long-term health care services for disabled and elderly veterans.

Veteran's interest groups primarily interacted with Congress on formulating the veteran's bill. Much of the language in the VMHCA was taken from presentations made by veteran's organizations. The only proposal veteran's groups were opposed to co-payment increases. However, they compromised with legislators and the president via the Veteran's Administration. Consequently, veteran's co-payments have been increased. On the other hand, the majority of the measures recommended by interest groups, especially veteran's groups, were included in the legislation.

In addition to veteran's groups, governmental interest groups were also involved in the legislative process and the enactment of the 1999 veteran's legislation. Groups such as the National Association of State Veteran's Homes (NASVH) lobbied in favor of increased funding for state operated veteran's homes and state agencies that are often responsible for the implementation of veteran's medical care services. Federal funding increases allows these agencies and program administrators to better serve veterans who need nursing home care services. Therefore, the efforts of the National Association of State Veteran's Homes made it possible for program administrators to (1) increase available bed space, (2) renovate and improve the safety of nursing homes, (3) construct new nursing home facilities, and (4) improve the livelihood of disabled and elderly veterans.

State officials responsible for implementing VA programs charged that veteran's health care is a key issue of interest because they are responsible for providing medical treatment, nursing home facilities, and services to veterans and their families. Hence, much of the burden for implementing veteran's entitlements falls on VA officials in regional offices and state and local nursing home administrators. State organizations feared that the VA budget would not be inadequately appropriated. Therefore, they feared that states would have to bear the financial burden of veteran's health care services and construction of new veteran's nursing homes facilities. These groups lobbied Congress and the executive through their statements and testimonies before the House and Senate Committee on Veteran's Affairs, the House Subcommittee on Health and the House Subcommittee on Benefits. State and local nursing home administrators were successful in persuading the legislature and executive to increase funding for the construction of new facilities. The grant awards also benefit those agencies and states that wish to renovate existing State operated nursing home facilities. Hence, the viability of many aging buildings that house disabled and elderly veterans has been extended. These groups are able to make the necessary renovations to old and deteriorating buildings.

Furthermore, private interests were also involved in the passage of the Veteran's Millennium Health Care Act of 1999. Unlike other groups, private groups, (i.e., American Health Care Association (AHCA) and the Ocala Harborside Healthcare Nursing Home) forcefully lobbied the federal government for increased funding for services provided to veterans in "non-VA" treatment facilities. These groups worked together in a uniform manner to obtain increased federal appropriations for medical treatment provided to veterans by private hospitals and health care providers. Thus, the private interests of health care professionals and hospital administrators were instrumental in influencing the passage if the 1999 veteran's bill. The Veteran's Millennium Health Care Act included provisions to reimburse "non-VA" treatment centers for emergency care provided to veterans enrolled in the VA health care program. In addition, these groups also successfully influenced Congress and President Clinton to allow the Department of Veteran's Affairs to contract out long-term care services, nursing care services and other specialized medical care like chiropractic and mental health services.

Political Parties and Bipartisan Cooperation Among Legislators

The Republican and Democratic parties played an integral role in the passage of the Veteran's Millennium Health Care Act of 1999. The Republican Party gained control of the House and Senate following 1994 congressional elections. The party retained its political control in the 1998 elections. The Republican leadership worked with Democratic leadership to build a spirit of bipartisanship in the consideration of the veteran's bill. Consequently, the leadership included Democratic legislative proposals into the legislation. Members of the Democratic Party introduced amendments that:

1. establishes priority status for Purple Heart Recipients;
2. adds bronchiolo alveolar carcinoma to the list of cancers
3. recognized by the Veteran's Administration as a "service-connected" disability;
4. requires the VA to conduct several studies to develop programs that will use various health care alternatives;
5. requires the Veteran's Administration to reimburse hospitals and medical professionals for emergency treatment provided to veterans by "non-VA" medical facilities.

Democratic members where allowed to include the aforementioned proposals for a number of reasons. They were able to impress upon he Republican leadership the importance of these measures. Additionally, the president failed to articulate or suggest additions reform measures. Moreover, both parties received fervent support from the interest groups, i.e., American Legion, State Veteran's Homes Association and the American Health Care Association (AHCA), involved in the legislative process.

In essence, the bi-partisan approach to the Veteran's Millennium Health Care Act was not adversarial. This was evident in the behavior of both Republican and Democratic members of Congress. The role orientations of legislators were mixed. The vast majority of legislators supported the bipartisan bill and supported it on the chamber floor. The legislation passed by a 369-48 vote in the House of Representatives. The bill passed by unanimous consent in the Senate. Although the majority of legislators acted in a "bipartisan" role orientation, forty-eight rank-and-file members assumed the "party indifferent" role orientation towards the veteran's bill. Many of those who opposed the legislation believed it did not do enough to redress veteran's concerns.

In conclusion, the political parties were effective in their interaction within the legislature. This is primarily due to the "bipartisan" role orientation of Democratic and Republican legislators coupled with strong institutional support for veterans and veteran's organizations. As such, the interaction between legislators and external participants (i.e., The State Veteran's Home Association, American Legion, Paralyzed Veterans of America (VVA), and American Health Care Association) helped ensure the enactment of the VMHCA.

The Interaction of Congressional Committees and the "Non-Partisan" Role Orientation of Legislators

The House and Senate Veteran's Affairs Committees assumed an important role in interacting within the legislative structure. During the first session of the 106th Congress, the House Republicans initially sponsored the bi-partisan bill. Representative Cliff Stearns, also a veteran, introduce the Act on June 9, 1999. The legislation was considered in the House Committee on Veteran's Affairs, the Subcommittee on Hospitals and Health and the Subcommittee on Benefits. Stearns (R-FL) served as chairman of the House Veteran's Affairs Subcommittee on Hospitals and Health. In addition, Representative Lane Evans (D- IL) also authored language included in the comprehensive veteran's bill. Democrats only opposed one provision designed to give the VA discretion over increasing veteran's co-payments for non-compensable service connected disabilities. Democratic members of the House and veteran's interest groups maintained that veterans were already finding it difficult to pay the then existing copayments for VA medical treatment and prescriptions. Ultimately, the Democrats were convinced that the increases would be necessary if the federal government were to mandate the VA to: (1) increase veteran's access to facilities and services, (2) expand long-term medical care services, and (3) reimburse "non-VA" treatment centers for emergency care given those veterans enrolled in the VA health care delivery system.

The Republicans and Democrats used a very cunning and astute approach to redressing veteran's issues. Undoubtedly, the impending 2000 congressional elections helped propel the parties to work together in a concerted effort to "fast-track" the veteran's bill. As such, the Republican leadership embraced legislative measures drafted by their Democratic counterparts to be incorporated into the massive veteran's reform legislation. This technique virtually ensured the passage of the Veteran's Millennium Health Care Act in the House of Representatives.

Members of the Senate approached the legislative proposal in a similar manner. The Senate Committee on Veteran's Affairs favorably reported the bill with an amendment. Senator Arlen Specter (R-PA) sponsored the amendment, but included legislative measures drafted by Democratic members like Senator Charles "Chuck" Robb of Virginia, and Senator J. Rockefeller of West Virginia. The Senate Amendment to H.R. 2116 - the Veteran's Millennium Health Care Act further strengthened the reform bill by establishing priority status for recipients of the Purple Heart Award and extending the viability of several veteran's cemetaries.

There only existed mild ideological disagreements between Republican and Democratic members of Congress. Through bi-partisan cooperation, the veteran's bill garnered the support of 20 co-sponsors ten (10) Republicans and ten (10) Democrats. The fact that both parties were willing and able to put ideological differences aside is linked to the strong sentiment shared by the public for America's veterans. The bi-partisan bill was met with very little resistance. The House and Senate Republican majorities were able to obtain more than the required votes to pass the legislation.

Furthermore, members of Congress communicated with President William Jefferson Clinton. Several of the provisions like emergency health care coverage evolved from statements the president issued on the state of health care during his 1992 presidential campaign. Much of the communication with the executive branch occurred between members of Congress and high ranking appointed bureaucrats in the Department of Veteran's Affairs.

As previously stated, when analyzing the interaction of the political parties, Republican leadership worked side by side with Democratic leaders in a bi-partisan manner. There were few occasions when the parties disagreed on legislative proposals to be added to the Veteran's Millennium Health Care Act. In most cases, the Republican majority compromised with Democratic committee members' suggestions to strengthen veteran's benefit programs.

The examination of committee deliberations indicates that the role orientations of committee and rank-and-file members were not heavily partisan. The support of committee members for the chairman and ranking members' proposals as well as the bi-partisan cooperation exhibited made it easy for Congress to pass the Veteran's Millennium Health Care Act (VMHCA).

The interaction between committee members and the rank-and-file membership of Congress was prompted into action by their need to create good policy and a desire to be re-elected in the 2000 congressional elections. The Veteran's Millennium Health Care Act, therefore, created an opportunity for members of Congress to successfully pass a major legislative measure before the conclusion of the first session of the 106th Congress.

It is this writer's contention that David Mayhew's theory partially explains the swift passage of the VMHCA. Members of the 106th Congress were partially motivated to work in a cooperative manner because of their desire to be re-elected. Thus, legislators worked in a manner that facilitated the passage of the veteran's reform bill. What's more, veteran's issues have been relegated to an elevated status in Congressional proceedings. Consequently, they wanted to make substantive contributions to the national legislature, i.e. committee service, specialization, and expertise, etc., and to show proof of "good service." Lastly, Congress virtually has an open door policy with veteran's groups. Hence, veteran's organizations have increased access to congressional leadership.

Notes

[1] Malcolm Jewell and Samuel Patterson, *The Legislative Process in the United States* (New York: Random House, 1977).

BIBLIOGRAPHY

Books

Bentley, Arthur. *The Process of Government*. Bloomington: The Principia Press, Inc., 1935.

Berry, Jeffrey. *Interest Group Society*. Boston: Little Brown and Company, 1989.

Berry, Jeffrey. *Lobbying for the People*. New Jersey: Princeton University Press, 1977.

Corwin, Edward S. *The President, Office and Powers 1787-1948*. New York: New York University Press, 1948.

Deering, Christopher and Steven Smith. *Congressional Politics*. Illinois: The Dorsey Press, 1969.

Edwards, George. *Presidential Influence in Congress*. San Francisco: W.H. Freeman and Company, 1980.

Fenno, Richard. *The Power of the Purse*. Boston: Little Brown and Company, 1966.

Fenno, Richard. *Congressmen in Committees*. Boston: Little Brown and Company, 1973.

Gray, Justin. *The Inside Story of the American Legion*. New York: Boni and Gaer, 1948.

Holtzman, Abraham. *Interest Group and Lobbying*. New York: MacMillan Company, 1966.

Jewell, Malcolm and Samuel Patterson. *The Legislative Process in the United States*. New York: Random House, 1977.

Key, V.O. *Politics, Parties and Pressure Groups*. 3rd ed. New York: Thomas Cromwell Company, 1952.

Key, V. O. *Public Opinion and Democracy.* New York: Alfred Knopf, 1961.

Laswell, Harold. *Democracy Through Public Opinion.* Wisconsin: George Banta Publishing, Company, 1941.

Light, Paul. *Forging Legislation.* New York: W.W. Norton and Company, 1992.

Lippman, Walter. *The Phantom Public.* New York: Harcourt Brace, 1925.

Lowell, A. Lawrence. *Public Opinion and Popular Government.* New York: Longmans Green and Company, 1926.

Mayhew, David. *Congress: The Electoral Connection.* Massachusetts: Yale University, 1974.

Neustadt, Richard. *Presidential Power.* New York: John Wiley and Sons, Inc., 1964.

O'Keefe, William and Morris Ogul. *The American Legislative Process.* 10th ed. New Jersey: Prentice Hall, 2001.

Olson, Manur. *The Logic of Collective Action: Public Goods and the Theory of Groups.* New York: Schocken Books, 1968.

Rosenthal, Alan. *The Third House: Lobbyists and Lobbying in the State.* Washington, D.C.: Congressional Quarterly Press, 1993.

Rossiter, Clinton Lawrence. *The American Presidency.* New York: Harcourt Brace, 1956.

Rossiter, Clinton Lawrence. *Parties and Politics in America.* New York: Cornell University Press, 1960.

Sabato, Larry. *Goodbye to Good-Time Charlie: The American Governor Transformed.* 2nd ed. Washington, D.C.: Congressional Quarterly Press, 1983.

Schneier, Edward and Bertram Gross. *Congress Today.* New York: St. Martin's Press, 1993.

Tatalovich, Raymond and Byron Daynes, *Presidential Power in the United States.* Belmont, California: Brooks Cole Publishing Company, 1984.

Truman, David. *The Governmental Process.* 1st ed. New York: Alfred A. Knopf, Inc., 1951.

Walton, Hanes. *Black Politics.* Philadelphia: Lippencott, 1972.

U.S. Constitution.

The Federalist Papers. Hammondsworth: Penguin, 1987.

Periodicals

Bach, Stanley. "House Rules Governing Committee Markup Procedures." Congressional Research Service. *Congressional Research Service* [database on-line] available from http://house.gov/rules/RL30244.pdf; Internet; accessed 5 July 2000.

Bach, Stanley. "Instructing House Conferees." *Congressional Research Service* [database on-line] available from http://www.house.gov/rules/98-381.htm; Internet; accessed 5 July 2000.

Brigman, William. "The Executive Branch and the Independent Regulatory Agencies." *Presidential Studies Quarterly* (Spring 1981), 244-246.

Hart, John. "Congressional Reaction to the White House." *Presidential StudiesQuarterly*. Vol. XI (Winter 1990): 83-91.

Hoff, Samuel. "The Presidential Pocket-Veto: Its Use and Legality." *Journal of Policy History*. Vol. VI (n.d. 1994), 188-208.

Neustadt, Richard. "Presidency and Legislation: Planning the President's Program," in *The Presidency*, ed. Aaron Wildavsky. Boston: Little Brown, 1969.

Pauly, Mark V. "Universal Health Insurance in the Clinton Plan: Coverage as a Tax-Financed Public Good." *Journal of Economic Perspectives, vol. 8, no. 3* (Summer 1994): 45-53.

Reynolds, William A. "Health Care reform: How Bright Prospects Plummeted." *The American College of Physicians Observer* (May1997) [on-line journal} available from http://www.acponline.org/journals/news/may97/plummet.htm; Internet; accessed 19 September 2001

Sachs, Richard. "Types of Committee Hearings." *Congressional Research Service* [database on-line] available from http://www.house.gov/rules/98-317.htm; Internet; accessed 5 July 2000.

Saturno, James. "Floor Consideration of Conference Reports in the House." *Congressional Research Service*, [database on-line] available from http://www.house.gov/rules/98-736.htm; Internet; accessed 5 July 2000.

Spitzer, Robert. "The Item Veto Dispute and Secular Crisis of the Presidency." *Presidential Studies Quarterly*. vol. XXVIII (Fall 1998):799-815.

Walker, Jack. "The Origins and Maintenance of Interest Groups in America. *American Political Science Journal.* Vol. 77, no. 2 (June 1983):390-406.
Wilson, Francis. "Concepts of Public Opinion." *The American Political Science Review.* vol. 27, no. 3 (June 1933):371-384.

Public Opinion Polls

Gallup Poll [Public Opinion on-line] (Storrs, Conneticut: University of Conneticut 1947-, accessed 30 October 2000); available from the Roper Center, Storrs, Conneticut, accession no. 0206707.
Gallup Poll [Public Opinion on-line] (Storrs, Conneticut: University of Conneticut 1947-, accessed 30 October 2000); available from the Roper Center, Storrs, Connecticut, accession no. 0206708.
Gallup Poll [Public Opinion on-line] (Storrs, Conneticut: University of Conneticut 1984-, accessed 30 October 2000); available from the Roper Center, Storrs, Conneticut, accession no. 0054382.
Gallup Poll [Public Opinion on-line] (Storrs, Conneticut: University of Conneticut 1991-, accessed 20 October 2000); available from the Roper Center, Storrs, Conneticut, accession no. 0043974.
Harris and Associates [Public Opinion on-line] (Storrs, Conneticut: University of Conneticut 1953 -, accessed 10 September 2001); available from the Roper Center, Storrs, Conneticut, accession no. 0033860.
Harris and Associates [Public Opinion on-line] (Storrs, Conneticut: University of Conneticut 1980 -, accessed 10 September 2001); available from the Roper Center, Storrs, Conneticut, accession no. 0355569.
Harris and Associates [Public Opinion on-line] (Storrs, Conneticut: University of Conneticut 1980 -, accessed 10 September 2001); available from the Roper Center, Storrs, Conneticut, accession 0355561.
Harris and Associates [Public Opinion on-line] (Storrs, Conneticut: University of Conneticut 1980 -, accessed 10 September 2001); available from the Roper Center, Storrs, Conneticut, accession no. 0355562.
Harris and Associates [Public Opinion on-line] (Storrs, Conneticut: University of Conneticut 1980 -, accessed 10 September 2001); available from the Roper Center, Storrs, Conneticut, accession no. 0355565.

Harris and Associates [Public Opinion on-line] (Storrs, Conneticut: University of Conneticut 1980 -, accessed 10 September 2001); available from the Roper Center, Storrs, Conneticut, accession no. 0004605.

Harris and Associates [Public Opinion on-line] (Storrs, Conneticut: University of Conneticut 1985 -, accessed 30 October 2000); available from the Roper Center, Storrs, Conneticut, accession no. 0059750.

Harris and Associates [Public Opinion on-line] (Storrs, Conneticut: University of Connecticut 1990 -, accessed 20 October 2001); available from the Roper Center, Storrs, Conneticut, accession no. 0141061.

Harris and Associates [Public Opinion on-line] (Storrs, Conneticut: University of Connecticut 1991 -, accessed 20 October 2001); available from the Roper Center, Storrs, Conneticut, accession no. 016812.

Harris and Associates [Public Opinion on-line] (Storrs, Conneticut: University of Connecticut 1995 -, accessed 30 October 2001); available from the Roper Center, Storrs, Conneticut, accession no. 0241760.

Los Angeles Times [Public Opinion on-line] (Storrs, Conneticut: University of Connecticut 1996-, accessed 20 October 2001); available from the Roper Center, Storrs, Conneticut, accession no. 0273013.

Mathew Greenwald Associates [Public Opinion on-line] (Storrs, Conneticut: University of Connecticut 1999-, accessed 20 October 2001); available from the Roper Center, Storrs, Conneticut, accession no. 0331549.

NBC News and Wall Street Journal [Public Opinion on-line] (Storrs, Conneticut: University of Connecticut 1996-, accessed 20 October 2001); available from the Roper Center, Storrs, Conneticut, accession no. 0270074.

Newspaper Articles

Dyhouse, Tim. "VFW – Backed Health Care Bill Approved." *VFW Washingtonwire* 9 August 1999 [database on-line] available from http://www.vfw.org/magazine/nov99/12.html; Internet; accessed 16 August 2000.

Dyhouse, Tim. "House to Vote on Health Care Reform Bill." *VFW*

Washingtonwire 19 September 1999 [database on-line] available from http://www.vfw.org/magazine/sep99/html; Internet; accessed 9 August 2000.

Eberhart, David. "VA Sets Rules for Purple Heart Recipients." *Stars and Stripes* 9 September 2000 [database on-line] available from http://www.stripes.com/servlet/News/ ViewArticle?articleId=100000293; Internet; accessed 30 September 200.

Hanchette, John. "Major Change in VA Policy Has American Legion Up in Arms." Arizona Republic, 17 October 1999, 14-15 (A).

Maddox, Jennifer. "Changes to Veteran's Care Sought Health: The House is Scheduled to Consider a Bill that Shifts Focus to Outpatient Clinics and Long-Term and Community Programs." *Orange County Register*, 27 July 1999, 5 (A).

Nesmith, Jeff. "Veterans Fight for Promise." *Dayton Daily News*, 15 March 2000, 1 (A).

Pratt, Mark. "Appeals Court Says Veterans Not Guaranteed Health Care." *The Plain Dealer*, 11 August 1999, 17 (A).

Snyer, Bill and Bonna de la Cruz. "Gore Wants Additional $1 Billion for Veterans, Critics Say Proposed Increases in Health Care Funding Fall Short." *The Tennessean*, 27 July 1999., 1 (A).

Steller, Chester. "Keeping the Faith with Veterans." *The Washington Post*, 18 August 1999, 18 (A).

Suro, Robert and Eric Peanin. "Battle Cry for Free Health Care: Retired Veterans Push Congress to Restore Promised Benefits." *The Washington Post*, 26 March 2000, 16 (A).

"Veterans Groups Sue Again." *The Augusta Chronicle*, 11 August 1999, 11 (C).

"Feds Work to Protect Vets' Healthcare." *Dayton Daily News*, 25 March 2000, 3 (A).

"Broken Promises." *St. Louis Post-Dispatch*, 18 August 1999, 6 (B).

"American Legion Sues Department of Veteran's Affairs." *U.S. Newswire*, 12 October 1999, 1 (A).

Public Documents

Clinton, President of the United States, et al. v. City of New York et al, [66 U.S.L.W. 4543].

U.S. Congress. House. Committee on Veteran's Affairs. *Appointment of Conferees toThe Veteran's Millennium Health Care Act.*

H.R. 2116. 106th Cong., 1st sess., *Congressional Record* (8 November 1999) vol. 145, no. 156, H11678.
U.S. Congress. House. Committee on Veteran's Affairs. Subcommittee on Health and Hospitals. *Cost of Estimates for H.R. 2116, The Veteran's Millennium Health Care Act.* 106th Cong., 1st sess., 30 June 1999.
U.S. Congress, House, Committee on Veteran's Affairs, Subcommittee on Hospitals and Health, *Cost Estimates for the Veteran's Millennium Health Care Act*, H.R. 2116, Report by Paul Van de Water, 106th Cong., 1st sess., 30 June 1999.
U.S. Congress. House. Committee on Veteran's Affairs. Subcommittee on Benefits. *Hearing on H.R. 605, H.R. 690, H.R. 784, H.R. 1212 and H.R. 1765.* H.R. 784. 106th Cong., 1st sess., 10 June 1999.
U.S. Congress. House. Committee on Veteran's Affairs. Subcommittee on Benefits. *Hearing on H.R. 605, H.R. 690, H.R. 784, H.R. 1212 and H.R. 1765.* H.R. 784. 106th Cong., 1st sess., 10 June 1999.
U.S. Congress. House. Committee on Veteran's Affairs. Subcommittee on Benefits. *Hearing on H.R. 1247, H.R. 1476, H.R. 1603, and H.R. 1633.* H.R. 1247. 106th Cong. 1st sess., 16 June 1999.
U.S. Congress. House. Committee on Veteran's Affairs. Subcommittee on Benefits. *Hearing on H.R. 1247, H.R. 1476, H.R. 1603, and H.R. 1633.* H.R. 1633. 106th Cong., 1st sess., 16 June 1999.
U.S. Congress. House. Committee on Veteran's Affairs. Subcommittee on Benefits. *Hearing on H.R. 1247, H.R. 1476, H.R. 1603, and H.R. 1633.* H.R. 1476. 106th Cong., 1st sess., 16 June 1999.
U.S. Congress. House. Committee on Veteran's Affairs. Subcommittee on Health and Hospitals. *The Impact of Budget Shortfalls on the Delivery of Health Care to Rural Veteran's.* 100th Congress., 1st sess., 2 December 1988.
U.S. Congress. House. Committee on Veteran's Affairs. Subcommittee on Health and Hospitals. *Planning, Budgeting and Management of Capital Assets.* Report prepared by Thomas Garthwaite. 106th Cong., 1st sess., 10 March 1999.
U.S. Congress. House. Committee on Veteran's Affairs. Subcommittee on Health and Hospitals. *The Proposed*

Veteran's Millennium Health Care Act. 106th Cong., 1st sess., 19 May 1999.

U.S. Congress. House. Committee on Veteran's Affairs. Subcommittee on Health and Hospitals. *The Proposed Veteran's Millennium Health Care Act.* Report prepared by Kenneth Kizer, 106th Cong., 1st sess., 1999.

U.S. Congress. House. Committee on Veteran's Affairs. *VA Health Care: Capital Asset Planning and Budgeting Needs Improvement.* Report prepared by Stephen Backhus. 106th Congress., 1st sess., 1999 [on-line database] available from http//veterans.house.gov/hearings/schedule106/mar99/3-10-99HEA/goa.htm; Internet; accessed 5 February 2000.

U.S. Congress. House. Committee on Veteran's Affairs. Subcommittee on Health and Hospitals. T*he Veteran's Millennium Health Care Act.* Report prepared by Stephen Backhus. 106th Cong., 1st sess., 19 March 1999.

U.S. Congress. House. Committee on Veteran's Affairs. Subcommittee on Health and Hospitals. *The Veteran's Millennium Health Care Act.* 106th Cong., 1st sess., 9 June 1999.

U.S. Congress. House. Committee on Veteran's Affairs. Subcommittee on Health and Hospitals. *The Veteran's Millennium Health Care Act.* Mark-Up of H.R. 2116. 106th Cong., 1st sess., 9 June 1999.

U.S. Congress. House. Committee on Veteran's Affairs. Subcommittee on Health and Hospitals. *The Veteran's Millennium Health Care Act.* Mark-Up of H.R. 2116. 106th Cong., 1st sess., 15 June 1999.

U.S. Congress. House and Senate. Committee on Veteran's Affairs. Subcommittee on Health and Hospitals. *The Veteran's Millennium Health Care Act.* Conference Report 106th Cong., 1st sess., 19 November 1999.

U.S. Congress. House. Committee on Veteran's Affairs. The Veteran's Millennium Health Care Act. Roll Call Vote 427. 106th Cong., 1st sess., *Congressional Record* (21 September 1999) [database on-line] available from http://clerkweb.house.gov/cgi-bin/vote.exe?year=1999&rollnumber=427; Internet; accessed 5 July 2000.

U.S. Congress. House. Committee on Veteran's Affairs. *VA Health Care Collections Fall Short of Expectations.* Report by

Stephen Backhus. 106th Cong., 1st sess. 1999. [database on-line] available from http://veterans.house/gov/hearings/schedules106/sept99/9-23-99/gao.htm; Internet; accessed 29 April 2000.

U.S. Congress. House. Committee on Veteran's Affairs. Subcommittee on Health and Hospitals. *Veteran's Health Administration*. Report by Thomas Gaithwaite, 106th Cong., 1st sess., 1999 [database on-line] available from http://veterans.house.gov/hearings/schedule106/mar99/3-10-9HEA/va.htm; Internet; accessed 29 April 2000.

U.S. Congress. House. Committee on Veteran's Affairs. *Proposed Legislation – Veteran's Millennium Health Care Act*. Report by Kenneth Kizer. 106th Cong., 1st sess., 1999 [database on-line] available from http://veterans.house.gov/hearings/ schedules106/may99/5-19-99/dva.htm; Internet; accessed 28 May 2000.

U.S. Congress. House. Committee on Veteran's Affairs. Subcommittee on Oversight and Investigations. *National Cemeteries, State Veteran's Cemeteries and Arlington National Cemetery*. Report by Colonel Robert F. Norton. 106th Cong., 1st sess., 1999 [database on-line] available from http://www.house.gov/va/hearings/schedule106/may99/5020-99OI/troa.htm; Internet; accessed 1 April 2000.

U.S. Congress, House. Committee on Veteran's Affairs. "Veteran's Affairs Committee Member List." 106th Cong., 1st sess., [database on-line] available from http://www.veterans.house.gov/committee.html; Internet; accessed 5 February 2000.

U.S. Congress, House, Committee on Veteran's Affairs, Subcommittee on Hospitals and Health, "Veteran's Affairs Subcommittee Member List," 106th Cong., 1st sess., [database on-line] available from http://www.veterans.house.gov/about/committee/subcom.htm; Internet; accessed 5 February 2000.

U.S. Congress. House. Committee on Veteran's Affairs. Subcommittee on Health and Hospitals. *Long Term Care Issues*. Report by Robert Shaw. 106th Cong., 1st sess., 1999 [database on-line] available from http://www.house.gov/va/hearings/schedule106/apr99/4-22-99/nasvh.htm; Internet; accessed 29 April 2000.

U.S. Congress. House. Representative Eva Clayton of North Carolina speaking for the Veteran's Millennium Health Care Act. H.R. 2116. 106th Cong., 1st sess., *Congressional Record* (23 2117. September 1999), vol. 145, no. 125, E1947.

U.S. Congress. House. Representative Michael Doyle of Pennsylvania speaking for the Veteran's Millennium Health Care Act. Conference Report 106-470. 106th Cong., 1st sess., *Congressional Record* (16 November 1999), vol. 145, no. 162, E2453.

U.S. Congress. House. Representative Bob Filner of California speaking for the Veteran's Millennium Health Care Act. H.R. 2116. 106th Cong., 1st sess., *Congressional Record* (5 August 2117. 1999) vol. 145, no. 114, E1784.

U.S. Congress. House. Representative Steny Hoyer of Maryland speaking for the Veteran's Millennium Health Care Act. H.R. 2116. 106th Cong., 1st sess., *Congressional Record* (4 October 1999) vol. 145, no. 133, E2023.

U.S. Congress. House. Representative Sheila Jackson-Lee speaking for the Veteran's Millennium Health Care Act. Conference Report 106-470. 106th Cong., 1st sess., *Congressional Record* (18 November 1999) vol. 145, no. 164, E2435.

U.S. Congress. House. Representative Ron Packard of California speaking for the Veteran's Millennium Health Care Act. H.R. 2116. 106th Cong., 1st sess., *Congressional Record* (22 2117. September 1999) vol. 145, no. 124, E1921.

U.S. Congress. House. Representative Harold Rogers of Kentucky speaking for the Veteran's Millennium Health Care Act. H.R. 2116. 106th Cong., 1st sess., *Congressional Record* (24 2117. September 1999) vol. 145, no. 126, E1956-1957.

U.S. Congress. House. Representative Christopher Smith of New Jersey speaking for the Veteran's Millennium Health Care Act. Conference Report 106-470. 106th Cong., 1st sess., *Congressional Record* (16 November 1999) vol. 145, no. 162, E2531.

U.S. Congress. House. Representative Cliff Stearns of Florida speaking for the Veteran's Millennium Health Care Act. H.R. 2116. 106th Cong., 1st sess., *Congressional Record* (15 June 1999) vol. 145, no. 84, H4228.

U.S. Congress. House. Representative Cliff Stearns of Florida speaking for the Veteran's Millennium Health Care Act. H.R. 106th Cong., 1st sess., *Congressional Record* (3 August

1999) vol. 145, no. 112, H6845-6846.

U.S. Congress. House and Senate. Joint Committee on Veteran's Affairs, Subcommittee on Hospitals and Health, *The Impact of Budget Shortfalls on the Delivery of Health Care to Rural Veterans*, 100th Cong., 1st sess., 2 December 1988.

U.S. Congress. Committee on Veteran's Affairs. Subcommittee on Hospitals and Health. *VA Health Care: Planning, Budgeting and Management of Capital Assets.* Report by Stephen Backhus. 106th Cong., 1st sess., 1999 [database on-line] available from http://veterans.house.gov/hearings/schedule106/mar99/3-10-99HEA/goa.htm; Internet; accessed 5 February 2000.

U.S. Congress, House. Committee on Veteran's Affairs. Subcommittee on Hospitals and Health. *The Veteran's Millennium Health Care Act.* H.R. 2116. Report by Stephen Backhus. 106th Cong., 1st sess., [database on-line] available from http://veterans.house.gov/hearings/schedule106/may99/5-19-99HEA/gao.htm; Internet; accessed 5 February 2000.

U.S. Congress. House and Senate. Joint Committee on Veteran's Affairs. Subcommittee on Health and Hospitals. *The Proposed Veteran's Millennium Health Care Act.* Report by Michael Berman, 106th Cong., 1st sess., 1999.

U.S. Congress. House and Senate. Joint Committee on Veteran's Affairs. Subcommittee on Health and Hospitals. *The Proposed Veteran's Millennium Health Care Act.* Report by John Daly. 106th Cong., 1st sess., 1999 [database on-line] available from http://www.house.gov/va/hearings/schedule106/may99/5-19-99/trea.htm;; Internet; accessed 1 August 2000.

U.S. Congress. House. Committee on Veteran's Affairs. Subcommittee on Hospitals and Health. *VA Health Care: Planning, Budgeting and Management of Capital Assets.* Report by Thomas Garthwaite. 106th Cong., 1st sess., 1999 [database on-line] available from http://veterans.house.gov/hearings/schedule106/mar99/3-10-99HEA/gao.htm; Internet; accessed 5 February 2000.

U.S. Congress. House. Committee on Veteran's Affairs. Subcommittee on Hospitals and Health. *The Proposed Veteran's Millennium Health Care Act.* Report by Kenneth Kizer. 106th Cong., 1st sess., 1999 [database on-line] available from http://veterans.house.gov/hearings/schedule106/mar99/5-19-99HEA/gao.htm; Internet; accessed 5 February 2000.

U.S. Congress. House and Senate. Joint Committee on Veteran's Affairs. Subcommittee on Health and Hospitals. *The Proposed Veteran's Millennium Health Care Act.* Report by Thomas A. Pouliot. 106th Cong., 1st sess., 1999.

U.S. Congress. House and Senate. Joint Committee on Veteran's Affairs. Subcommittee on Health and Hospitals. *The Proposed Veteran's Millennium Health Care Act.* Report by Roger Putnam. 106th Cong., 1st sess., 1999 [database on-line] available from http://www.veterans.house.gov/hearings/schedule106/mar99/3-4-99/ncoa.htm; Internet; accessed 29 April 2000.

U.S. Congress. House and Senate. Joint Committee on Veteran's Affairs. Subcommittee on Health and Hospitals. *The Proposed Veteran's Millennium Health Care Act.* Report by Robert Shaw, 106th Cong., 1st sess., 1999.

U.S. Congress. House and Senate. Joint Committee on Veteran's Affairs. Subcommittee on Health and Hospitals. *The Proposed Veteran's Millennium Health Care Act.* Report by Harley Thomas. 106th Cong., 1st sess., 1999 [database on-line] available from http://www.veterans.house.gov/va/hearings/schedule106/5-19-99/pva.htm; Internet; accessed 1 April 2000.

U.S. Congress. House and Senate. Joint Committee on Veteran's Affairs. Subcommittee on Health and Hospitals. *The Proposed Veteran's Millennium Health Care Act.* Report by Steve Watson. 106th Cong., 1st sess., 1999 [database on-line] available from http://www.veterans.house.gov/hearings/schedule106/apr99/4-22-99/ahca.htm; Internet; accessed 29 April 2000.

U.S. Congress. House and Senate. Joint Committee on Veteran's Affairs. Subcommittee on Health and Hospitals. *The Veteran's Millennium Health Care Act.* Report by Richard Weidman. 106th Cong., 1st sess., 1999 [database on-line] available from http:www.veterans.house.gov/hearings/schedule106/may99/5-19-99/vva.htm; Internet; accessed 1 April 2000.

U.S. Congress. Senate. Senator Pete Domenici of New Mexico speaking for the Veteran's Millennium Health Care Act. Conference Report 106-470. 106th Cong., 1st sess.,

Congressional Record (23 September 1999), vol. 145, no. 125, S14905.

U.S. Congress. Senate. Senator John Rockefeller of West Virginia speaking for the Veteran's Millennium Health Care Act. Conference Report 106-470. 106th Cong., 1st sess., *Congressional Record* (19 November 1999) vol. 145, no. 165, S14906.

U.S. Congress. Senate. Senator Olympia Snowe of Maine speaking for the Veteran's Millennium Health Care Act. Conference Report 106-470. 106th Cong., 1st sess., *Congressional Record* (19 November 1999) vol. 145, no. 165, S14910.

U.S. Congress. Senate. Senator Arlen Specter of Pennsylvania speaking for the Veteran's Millennium Health Care Act. Conference Report 106-470. 106th Cong., 1st sess., *Congressional Record* (19 November 1999), vol. 145, no. 165, S14905.

U.S. Congress. Senate. "Message from the Senate." H.R.2116. 106th Cong., 1st sess., *Congressional Record* (8 November 1999) vol. 145, no. 156, H11648.

U.S. Congress. Senate. Committee on Veteran's Affairs. "Senate Veteran's Affairs Member List." 106th Cong., 1st sess., [database on-line} available from http://www.senate.gov/committees/; Internet; accessed 5 February 2000.

U.S. Congress. Senate. Committee on Veteran's Affairs. *Veteran's Millennium HealthCare Act*. Senate Amendment 2541. 106th Cong., 1st sess., *Congressional Record* (24 September 1999) vol. 145, no. 126, H11648.

U.S. Department of Veteran's Affairs. Office of Public Affairs. *Facts About the Department of Veteran's Affairs*. [Washington, D.C.]: U.S. Department of Veteran's Affairs, Veteran's Health Administration, 1999.

U.S. Department of Veteran's Affairs. Office of Public Affairs. *VA History in Brief*. [Washington, D.C.]: U.S. Department of Veteran's Affairs, Veteran's Health Administration, 1999.

U.S. President Clinton. Proclamation. "On Signing the Veteran's Millennium Health Care and Benefits Act." *Federal Register* (30 November 1999) vol. 64, no. 2, Microfiche.

U.S. President. *Public Papers of the Presidents of the United States*. (Washington, D.C.: Office of the Federal Register, National Archives and Records Service, 1993. William Jefferson

Clinton. 1993.
U.S. President. *Public Papers of the Presidents of the United States.* Washington, D.C.: Office of the Federal Register, National Archives and Records Service, 1999. William Jefferson Clinton. 1999.

Statutes

Dependence Pension Act. Statutes at Large. Vol. 26 (1890).
Disabled Veterans Rehabilitation Act. Statutes at Large. Vol. 43 (1949).
Homestead Act. Statutes at Large. Vol. 12 (1862).
Omnibus Budget Reconciliation Act . Statutes at Large. Vol. 104 (1990).
Post-Vietnam War Veterans Educational Assistance Act. Statutes at Large. Vol. 90 (1979).
Selective Training Act. Statutes at Large. Vol. 54 (1940).
Servicemen's Readjustment Act. Statutes at Large. Vol. 58 (1944).
Sherwood Act. Statutes at Large. Vol. 37 (1912).
Veteran's Benefits Improvement Act. Statutes at Large. Vol. 110 (1996).
Veteran's Compensation Cost-of Living Adjustment Act. Statutes at Large. Vol. 110 (1996).
Veteran's Health Care Amendments Act. Statutes at Large. Vol. 93 (1979).
Veteran's Millennium Health Care Act. Statutes at Large. Vol. 113 (1999).
Veteran's Readjustment Act. Statutes at Large. Vol. 72 (1958).
Morton v. West [12 Vet. App. 477 (1999)].

About the Author

La Trice M. Washington is a Professor of American Government at Otterbein College. She is a recent graduate of Howard University where she earned her Ph.D. in American Government and Public Administration in May 2002. She received her M.A. in American Government from the University of Virginia in 1994. She is a Summa Cum Laude graduate of St. Augustine's College and earned her B.A. in Political Science in 1991. She is also a contributing author for Encyclopedia on Affirmative Action published by Oryx Press/Greenwood Press. The reference guide addresses milestone legislative measures, Executive Orders, case law, significant organizations and individuals involved in the debate over affirmative action. She has received numerous honors and awards including Who's Who Among America's Teachers, 2001-2002, Metropolitan Area Charter Schools (MAC) Teacher of the Year 2001, National Aeronautics Space Administration (NASA) Public Service Intern, 1998, Virginia Governor's Fellowship 1991-1992,Virginia Council of Higher Education Graduate Fellowship 1992-1994, American Political Science Association Fellow, 1991, Summa Cum Laude Graduate, Saint Augustine's College, 1991, American Political Science Association Ralph Bunche Scholar, 1990, and the American Political Science Association Summer Research Grant, 1990. She is currently researching voter apathy and its impact on public policy formulation and democracy in the United States.

She can be reached at lwashington@otterbein.edu.

INDEX

www.ingramcontent.com/pod-product-compliance
Ingram Content Group UK Ltd.
Pitfield, Milton Keynes, MK11 3LW, UK
UKHW012034150926
475560UK00001B/5

9 780761 826651